LAZARUS, COME FORTH

Discover God's plan to restore what the devil took from you

Jonathan Omajali

KINGDOM BOOKS

Published by Kingdom Books, an imprint of *CreativeJuicesBooks, Singapore (www.creativejuicesbooks.com)*

National Library Board, Singapore Cataloguing–in–Publication Data

Name: Omajali, Jonathan.

Title: Lazarus, come forth : discover God's plan to restore what the devil took from you / Jonathan Omajali.

Description: Singapore : Kingdom Books, [2020]

Identifier(s): OCN 1137082974 | ISBN 978-981-14-4729-7 (paperback)

Subject(s): LCSH: Christian life. | Spiritual life--Christianity. | God (Christianity)

Classification: DDC 248.4--dc23

Contents

DEDICATION

To the late Reverend James Omajali:
A father, a mentor, and a faithful
soldier of Christ.

Preface

Jesus said, "The thief comes only to steal and kill and destroy..." (*John 10:10*). The thief is after your Lazarus. Lazarus represents that which is precious to you: "the one you love" (*John 11:3*); it can be your marriage, family, loved ones, dreams, health, ministry, or means of livelihood. The devil's aim is to pounce on it and kill it, like he did in Bethany to the brother of Mary and Martha.

Today, many people are mourning and living in sorrow because the enemy has killed their Lazarus. For such individuals, there is little hope of having him back because of the enormity of the problem. Martha said to the Lord, "by this time he stinks" (*John 11:39, AKJV*). But don't despair. Christ's aim is to restore that which is dead: "Our friend Lazarus sleeps; but I go, that I may awake him out of sleep" (*John 11:11, AKJV*).

As you go through the following pages, you will not only discover God's plan to restore your Lazarus, you will also learn how to take back everything that the devil has stolen, killed or destroyed in your life.

This isn't just another book; it is a message of hope from the Lover of your soul, Jesus. God bless you.

Cover Picture:
The Raising of Lazarus
by Leon Bonnat, 1833-1922

1

The Long Wait

Strengthen the weak hands, and make firm the feeble knees. Say to those who are fearful-hearted, "Be strong, do not fear! Behold, your God will come with vengeance, with the recompense of God; He will come and save you."

Isaiah 35:3-4, NKJV

For four days, friends and family members flocked to the house of Mary and Martha. It was four days of agony, four days of mourning, and four days of wondering why God had to let Lazarus die so early.

"He was such a good man, a friend of Jesus," some would have said as they paid their tributes. They couldn't understand why God would allow Mary and Martha, whose house was one of Christ's House Fellowship centres, to go through such a terrible storm. The two sisters must have had their ears filled with words of comfort from sympathizers: "Take heart, Sister Mary, God knows why. We shall meet again on the resurrection morning. Be strong, Sister Martha, you can't continue to cry like those who do not have hope..."

Everyone came to condole with the bereaved family, but the person they needed most at this trying moment was yet to come. The sisters had sent for Him when Lazarus was ill, but He failed to turn up. They had waited for Him the day Lazarus died, hoping He would come and raise him from the dead—the way He had raised the son of the woman of Nain—but He failed to show up. When they couldn't wait for Him anymore, they finally buried Lazarus. This was the fourth day since the burial, and nobody in Bethany had caught sight of their friend Jesus. It was hard to explain how such a dear friend could have let them down after years of what was a perfect relationship.

How long has the Lord "stayed away" since your problem began? Perhaps ten years, twenty years, twenty-nine years? You expected Him to show up when you turned twenty, but He failed to come. He hasn't turned up yet, and you have already clocked thirty-eight. Most of your mates are already married but He still hasn't come to Bethany.

Or perhaps you expected Him to show up the moment you got married, but He failed to come. At your wedding, the MC said, "We shall be back in nine months' time to celebrate with the couple." You waited for nine months, one year, four years, ten years… and you are now approaching menopause, but still the Lord hasn't come to Bethany.

Or maybe you expected Him to show up the moment you left school and put in that application. You waited for the call after the interview, but it never came. Now it's been ages since you left school, and you are still jobless. You have worn out your shoes looking for work; you have prayed with all prayer and supplication; but He still hasn't come to Bethany.

David, facing a similar situation, cried, "I am worn out calling for help; my throat is parched. My eyes fail, looking for my God" (*Psalm 69:3*).

How long have you been waiting at Bethany? How many years have you lived with that ailment, fasting and trusting God? You have been prayed for, gone to the best hospitals…

and still nothing has changed. Maybe, like the woman with the issue of blood, you have spent all you had on hospital bills and false prophets. You have been waiting and waiting.

Mary and Martha were right where you are now—*left waiting at the bus stop.* The best that their loved ones could do was to offer words of sympathy. Sometimes, life and circumstances bring us to that point where the best that people can give us is a word of sympathy. For four days, friends of Mary and Martha tried to alleviate the trauma of the two sisters, but no word was strong enough to salvage the problem. No word had the potency to get to the root of the matter. The more they sympathized, the more the body of Lazarus decomposed in the grave. Not even their wailing and tributes could yank Lazarus from the terrible grip of death.

As sympathizers came and went, the two sisters kept their eyes on the road in anticipation of Christ's arrival. Like the Psalmist, they continued to wait until He showed up:

> Behold, as the eyes of servants look unto the hand of their masters, and as the eyes of a maiden unto the hand of her mistress; so our eyes wait upon the LORD our God, until that he have mercy upon us.
>
> *Psalm 123:2, KJV*

Have you been waiting? I have good news for you: the season of waiting is coming to an end. The Scriptures tell us that He came four days after Lazarus was buried. You are in your *fourth* day; it's time to get your Lazarus back. We have this assurance: "The eyes of all wait on you; and you give them their meat in due season" (*Psalm 145:15, AKJV*). This is the "season" you have been waiting for. Cheer up; He is restoring that which the enemy took from you.

He will come to save you

> Our friend Lazarus sleeps; but I go, that I may awake him out of sleep.
>
> *John 11:11, AKJV*

It took days before Jesus eventually made this important decision: "I go." By then, it already seemed like a pointless journey. The time the people needed Him to do something about Lazarus' condition had come and gone.

For some, this failure to come early showed how little He valued His relationship with Lazarus and his sisters. "If He really loved them, He would have hurried down to Bethany when they sent for Him," they would have said. But, you see, this same Lazarus was the first man that Jesus called "friend"—the same way Abraham was called "the friend of God" (*2 Chronicles 20:7; Isaiah 41:8; James 2:23*). So, it was a relationship that Jesus truly valued.

You may hear people say to you, "If this Jesus is truly your friend, why hasn't He come to your rescue? If this Jesus really loves you, as you claim He does, why hasn't He brought someone to marry you? If this Jesus—that you are always running after day and night—is truly a friend, why hasn't He taken away this poverty in your life? If this Jesus is a friend indeed, why are you going through all these problems?"

Now the Bible tells us clearly that, despite His delay and its consequences, "Jesus loved Martha and her sister and Lazarus" (*John 11:5*). The trip to Bethany was a dangerous one, because "a short while ago the Jews there tried to stone" Him (*John 11:8*). But He went all the same, because He truly loved Martha and her sister and Lazarus.

More than just a visit

I go, that I may awake him out of sleep.

John 11:11, AKJV

When others set off for Mary and Martha's home, they said, "I go to sympathize with those poor sisters over the death of their brother"; or, "I go to sign the condolence register"; or, "I go to give them some financial help with the burial arrangements and refreshments for the guests"; or, "I go to give them the letter from the Association of Jesus' Friends International". But, when Jesus said "I go", His agenda was to turn the people's mourning to laughter.

When Jesus says "I go" to your situation, it means He is coming with His solution: "your God is coming to destroy your enemies. He is coming to save you" (*Isaiah 35:4, NLT*). When He says "I go", it means it is time to put an end to your battle: "He makes wars cease to the ends of the earth" (*Psalm 46:9*). "I go" also means "I have had enough of my child's tears; it is time to restore what the devil has taken."

To some, His coming to Bethany was merely a condolence visit. But it was more than just that. It is important for us to understand this, so that we can look forward to every one of Christ's visitations. Don't mistake the Lord's visit for a condolence visit; it is a visit aimed at saving you and destroying your enemies. Lazarus had died, so it was logical for Mary and Martha to think the Lord's visit was just to cheer them up; but Christ's coming bore more promises and blessings than they could ever have imagined.

Do you know what God has in mind for you? You probably don't know the surprises He has in His package for you. Sarah thought a child from her maid was the best she could get, because she had passed the age of conceiving. But God had better plans for her. Joseph was merely looking for someone to get him out of prison; but little did he know that God's package for him was a throne in a land where he was considered a slave and a criminal.

His plans for you are more than you think. Your Lazarus may be in the grave, but He has surprises for you when He visits you in Bethany:

> Eye has not seen, nor ear heard, nor have entered into the heart of man the things which God has prepared for those who love Him.
>
> *1 Corinthians 2:9, NKJV*

The Lord Himself tells you, "I know the plans I have for you… plans to prosper you and not to harm you, plans to give you hope and a future" (*Jeremiah 29:11*). No one understood this truth more than David; no wonder he said:

> How precious are your thoughts about me, O God. They cannot be numbered! I can't even count them; they outnumber the grains of sand! And when I wake up, you are still with me!
>
> *Psalm 139:17-18, NLT*

Jesus is visiting you this very moment. Don't mistake His coming for another sympathy or condolence visit; it's a visit that will deal with the root of your problem. He is coming, even after four days. He is coming to save you and destroy your enemies. He is coming to get the prey out of the mouth of the devil. He is coming to clean up all the mess the devil has created. He is coming to get your Lazarus out of the grave, even though he already stinks. Quit crying and complaining. Quit saying, "Why me?" Lazarus will be out. Amen.

2

A Reason to Believe

Then said Martha unto Jesus, Lord, if thou hadst been here, my brother had not died. But I know, that even now, whatsoever thou wilt ask of God, God will give it thee.

John 11:21-22, KJV

This was a moment of intense sorrow. But, despite the gloom and the hopelessness of the situation, hope sprang up in the heart of Martha the moment she sighted Christ. For the first time, she began to sense that something good could still come out of her bleak situation. It was still possible to have Lazarus back, even though she had never experienced such a miracle.

She said to Jesus, "Things have really gone out of hand because of your delay, but it's still up to you. All it takes is for you to ask God." This was no ordinary statement; it was one that came by inspiration. As with Peter (*Matthew 16:17*), flesh and blood had not revealed this to her: that "whatsoever thou wilt ask of God, God will give it thee".

The Extraordinary Advocate

"Whatsoever you ask God, God will give it". What exactly was Martha saying to the Lord? She was drawing Christ's attention to His advocacy role. Later, John and Paul would shed light on this statement by Martha.

John said, "My dear children… we have an advocate with the Father—Jesus Christ, the Righteous One" (*1 John 2:1*). It is good to have an advocate. An advocate speaks in your favour and defends you in court. Sometimes you may have a very good case but won't know exactly how to defend yourself. You may not know the words to say to convince the judge. Or you may have a weak case that you are not likely to win. But, even if you have the worst case possible, the verdict can still swing in your favour—if you have a good advocate to defend you. The same principle applies in the spiritual realm. It is great to have an advocate like Christ.

Martha knew that Jesus could present their case in a way that would move the Father to bring Lazarus back to life. The Scriptures had already assured her that nothing is impossible with God: ""I know that You can do everything" (*Job 42:2, NKJV*). The issue now was getting a Man who had the ability to move God to bring a stinking body back to life. In Christ, Martha saw that Man—the Extraordinary Advocate. She saw the Advocate capable of persuading the Father to do the unimaginable. Was she right? Jesus proved she *was* right when He said, "I know that You always hear Me…" (*John 11:42, NKJV*).

Jesus was and is our Advocate. He didn't stop being our Advocate after His exit from earth. Paul assures us:

> Who then is the one who condemns? No one. Christ Jesus who died—more than that, who was raised to life—is at the right hand of God and is also interceding for us.
>
> *Romans 8:34*

He intercedes for us; put in another way, He is our Advocate, entreating and pleading with the Father on our behalf.

Therefore, he is able to save completely those who come to God through him, because he always lives to intercede for them.

Hebrews 7:25

You have an Extraordinary Advocate, and that is one reason you should be confident that you can have your Lazarus back. Your case may be terrible, it may look like a case you can never win in the court of heaven; but, with Jesus as your Advocate, you can rest in the assurance that the Father will swing the final judgment in your favour. You have a reason to believe you can have your Lazarus back.

Note the word she used: "whatsoever". That includes your case. He is capable of handling and winning any case. For Martha, at this point, the real issue was not the fact that Lazarus had died. The real issue was not the fact that he had been in the grave for four days and was already stinking. The real issue was whether the Lord was willing to ask the Father to do something about it.

Is Jesus interested in your case? This is the only thing that matters (*1 John 5:14-15*). A leper said to Jesus, ""Lord, if you are willing, you can make me clean" (*Matthew 8:2-3*). Jesus said, "Sure, I'm willing." You have a willing Father and an Extraordinary Advocate. There is therefore a reason to believe you can have your Lazarus back.

"I Know"

But I know, that even now, whatsoever thou wilt ask of God, God will give it thee.

John 11:22, KJV

One of the keys to this great miracle—Jesus raising Lazarus from the dead—lies in this simple expression, *"I know."*

What you know of the Lord is what will count in the days of adversity. It is not the number of titles you have or the number of years you have spent in Church: "but the people who know their God shall be strong, and carry out *great exploits*" (*Daniel 11:32, NKJV*). To have the strength for great exploits in the days of adversity, you must *know* your God. If you want to have your Lazarus back from the grips of the devil, you must *know* your God. Knowing God is crucial to receiving what He plans to give you. Many Israelites never made it to the Promised Land because God swore in His wrath, "They shall never enter my rest" (*Hebrews 3:11*). God swore and made such a far-reaching decision because those people did not know Him:

> Therefore I was angry with that generation, and said, "They always go astray in their heart, and they have not known My ways."
>
> *Hebrews 3:10, NKJV*

God said, "I can't walk with these people, I can't take them to the Promised Land. They have seen my mighty power and my goodness, but they still don't know me and my ways. It is better that they perish here in the wilderness. I prefer to walk with a new generation that knows my ways."

Today, we have people who have been in the church for ages, but they don't know the Lord. God is looking for people who know Him, so that He can bless them. In *Matthew 8:5-13*, we find the story of a centurion who came to Jesus, beseeching Him to heal his servant who was sick and grievously tormented. Jesus got ready to go, but the centurion stopped Him. He told the Lord, "You don't need to come. I'm not worthy that you should come under my roof. Speak the word only, and my servant shall be healed."

A journey that probably would have taken Jesus an hour was cut short. The healing of the servant also came earlier than expected. Why? Because this centurion knew the ways of the Lord. He knew that, when it comes to exercising authority, you don't have to be physically present; you only need to issue a word and those concerned will obey. He recognized Jesus as a man of authority, with angels and demons under His control (*Colossians 1:16*). He knew that a word from Jesus was enough to cast out the evil spirit troubling his servant at home. So, he said, "Lord, why bother? A word would do the job." This centurion knew the ways of the Lord.

Psalm 115:3 says, "Our God is in heaven; he does whatever pleases him." He doesn't have to come down. Right there in heaven, He issues His word, and those individuals and problems concerned obey accordingly.

Martha said, "I know." How did she know? I have already said it came by revelation. But this revelation was only possible because of her acquaintance with the Lord. The Bible tells us that "a certain woman named Martha received him into her house" (*Luke 10:38-42, KJV*).

That word "certain" could refer to many of us who have received Jesus into our lives. But it is not enough to receive Him into your house by giving your life to Him. When Martha received Him into her house, she became involved in serving. But Jesus told her, "You are jumping about, trying to please me with your service. But that's not what is most important. One thing is needful: sitting at my feet, learning of me, and absorbing my words, as your sister is doing. This is what you need most."

This admonition must have changed Martha's orientation and, from that moment onward, the paramount thing in her life was listening to Christ and getting acquainted with Him.

This was the root of her revelation. It was from this spring of accumulated words—which she had absorbed from the Lord — that the Holy Spirit could remind her of things from above:

> "But the Helper, the Holy Spirit, whom the Father will send in My name, He will teach you all things, and bring to your remembrance all things that I said to you."
>
> *John 14:26, NKJV*

Many people only want to be prayed for. They want hands laid on them. Spare them the Word. Spare them all that talk from the Bible. No time for that. Just pour anointing oil on them and let their troubles vanish. No! That won't help you when the devil comes for your Lazarus. What will prove invaluable, when you want your Lazarus back from the grips of the enemy, are the times you spend at the feet of the Lord, listening to Him and getting acquainted with Him.

On Sundays, many churchgoers come into the Lord's presence for a while; but, after that, it's goodbye to Him. They are encumbered with their businesses. You won't see them in Bible Studies. You won't see them spending time with the Holy Spirit, studying the Word. So, when the devil comes for their Lazarus, it is hard for them to say to God, "I know." You need your Lazarus back? Get acquainted with the Lord. That's when you too can say to the Lord, *"I know."*

Acquaintance with the Lord brings peace; "thereby good will come to you" (*Job 22:21-23, NKJV*). The devil brought evil to the two sisters, but good came afterwards. They laid up the Word of God in their hearts, and the Word became the bedrock for their miracle.

In *Job 19:1-29*, we see Job going through his toughest time. His soul had been vexed with the words of his friends.

His glory was gone. His closest friends had failed him. Even his servant wouldn't answer him. His breath had become strange to his wife. But, amidst his travail, he spoke out:

"But as for me, I *know* that my Redeemer lives, and he will stand upon the earth at last. And after my body has decayed, yet in my body I will see God!"

Job 19:25-26, NLT

There was something that kept Job going until his salvation came: *"I know that my Redeemer lives!"* That knowledge was enough to keep him afloat in the midst of his storm.

What do you know of the Lord? If all you know is how to ask for manna from above and cry out in anger when you are thirsty, then you have to get back to His feet—like Mary and Martha—and begin to get acquainted with Him. If all you do is to put in an appearance in church on Sunday, just to keep the Sabbath Day holy, then you need to get back to the feet of the Lord and begin to receive and lay up His words in your heart. It will be hard to have your Lazarus back when you can't say to the Lord, "I know."

When He fails to show up early, you should be able to say "I know." He will come because He lives. When He shows up after your Lazarus is gone, you should still be able to say to Him, "I *know* that all things are possible with you."

Don't spend any more nights worrying; spend them getting to know Him. Don't spend any more time telling people about what the enemy has been doing to you; spend those times getting to know Him. Lay up His Word in your heart and start telling Him, "Lord, I *know...*" Your miracle will be next. Amen.

3

The Master Is Come

She saith unto him, Yea, Lord: I believe that thou art the Christ, the Son of God, which should come into the world. And... she went her way, and called Mary her sister secretly, saying, The Master is come, and calleth for thee.

John 11:27-28, KJV

"The Master is come, and calleth for thee." This was the news Martha gave her sister Mary. What she said here raises a number of issues that we need to come to grips with:

He Is Come

Why did He come? Firstly, He came because *He is a faithful God.* Secondly, He came because they sent for Him. It is inconsequential whether He came the very moment they sent for Him or not. What is important is the result of His coming. Why did He come? He came because He promised that, if we call to Him, He will answer us (*Jeremiah 33:3*). He came because He promised that He will never leave us nor forsake us (*Hebrews 13:5*). He came because He said He is our refuge in the days of trouble (*Psalm 46:1*). That is faithfulness. God is a faithful God (*Revelation 19:11*).

In our walk with the Lord, this very thought must be ingrained in our spirit—*that God is faithful.* He may delay for four days, but it doesn't change the fact that He is a faithful God who will eventually show up.

Many believe God is holy and mighty, but they are not sure if He is faithful. Oftentimes we go through experiences that can make us question the faithfulness of God. Terrible things happen to us, and the question that pops up in our minds is, "Where is God in all of this?" But *1 Corinthians 1:9* assures us that "God is faithful, who has called you into fellowship with his Son, Jesus Christ our Lord."

Always bear this in mind if you want to have a smooth walk with the Lord—*He is faithful.* It is important that you keep on saying this to yourself, even when the situation doesn't seem like He is a faithful God. Take the example of Job who, in all his sufferings, could say this of God:

> "Look, I go forward, but He is not there, and backward, but I cannot perceive Him; when He works on the left hand, I cannot behold Him; when He turns to the right hand, I cannot see Him. But He knows the way that I take; when He has tested me, I shall come forth as gold.
>
> *Job 23:8-10, NKJV*

It must have been very troubling for Job to seek the Lord on the left, right, back and forth, and still end up not finding Him. But, right in the midst of all this, he knew that God hadn't abandoned or betrayed him. Our knowledge and our belief in the faithfulness of God will always serve as an anchor in the midst of the storm. The moment you take your hold off this anchor, you will begin to sink.

Job said, "I shall come forth as gold." Why? Because he believed God was too faithful to leave him in the mess. He knew God was at work; He was in the process of turning his adversities into gold. Sometimes we may not see God; that's because He is working on turning our adversities into gold.

He is working behind the scenes. With this mindset of God being faithful, Job declared, "… all the days of my appointed time will I wait, till my change come" (*Job 14:14b, KJV*).

Each time the devil attacks us, his aim is to discredit God; to make Him look like an unfaithful Father. "Where is the fulfilment of His promises to you?" he sneers. The moment we believe his allegation—that God is not really as faithful as the Bible says—we have already lost ground in our battle with the enemy. Say instead to yourself, "God is faithful." Lazarus may be in the grave, but God is faithful. He may be stinking by now, but God is faithful. Paul exhorts us:

> No temptation has overtaken you except what is common to mankind. And God is faithful; he will not let you be tempted beyond what you can bear. But when you are tempted, he will also provide a way out so that you can endure it.
>
> *1 Corinthians 10:13*

God is faithful, and He wants us to walk in the light of this knowledge. Many Israelites who left Egypt never made it to the Promised Land—because they doubted God's faithfulness. They even accused Him of bringing them into the wilderness to die by the sword; this is what they said:

> "Why is the LORD taking us to this country only to have us die in battle? Our wives and our little ones will be carried off as plunder! Wouldn't it be better for us to return to Egypt?"
>
> *Numbers 14:3, NLT*

Do you know what they were saying in essence? They were saying that God lured them out of Egypt into the wilderness only to have them killed there. How unfaithful they must have imagined God to be! After all the mighty deeds in Egypt and the great deliverance at the Red Sea, they still wouldn't accept God as their faithful Father—the same way many of us tend to doubt God's faithfulness, despite the fact that He loved us so much that He gave us His Son Jesus.

Martha said, "The Master has come. He hasn't abandoned us. He hasn't left us in the lurch. He hasn't left us at the mercy of the devil. The Master is come!"

"The Master is come, and He calls for you." God's Word tells us that "He who calls you is faithful, who also will do it" (*1 Thessalonians 5:24, NKJV*).

He Is the Master

Prior to Jesus' arrival, Satan held sway and was hailed as the master. He brought sickness and death to Lazarus, thereby striking sorrow into the hearts of Mary and Martha. It takes a master to do all of that, and it takes a greater Master to undo all of that.

The devil will do everything possible to make us see him as the master. Threats, lies and calamities are just a few of his tools. He wants to put us in awe of him. He wants to put us to flight. But we need not fear him, for he is not the real master. Instead, we should respond as David did, when he said, "In the LORD I put my trust; how can you say to my soul, 'Flee as a bird to your mountain'?" (*Psalm 11:1, NKJV*)

When Jesus showed up, He was prepared to erase the people's doubts about who was really the Master. There might have been arguments about His Lordship, but this time He came to clear the people's doubts. You may have some issues which are claiming lordship over your life, but today the real Master will dislodge them all and restore your joy.

Some of the mourners present said, ""Could not this Man, who opened the eyes of the blind, also have kept this man from dying?" (*John 11:37, NKJV*) They knew Jesus to be the Master when it came to opening the eyes of the blind. They knew Him as the Master when it came to stopping people from dying. They knew Him as the Master when it came to teaching the Word of God as a Rabbi. They were not sure, however, if He was the Master when it came to bringing a decomposing body back to life.

There is always a dimension of God's power that you haven't seen yet. He isn't just the Master in some situations; He is the Master in all situations. With Him, "nothing shall be impossible" (*Luke 1:37, KJV*). The devil might be telling you, "Yes, God healed that sister, but her case is not as terrible as yours. Yes, God delivered that man, but his condition is not as terrible as yours."

Well, Jesus is not just the Master of some situations; He is the Master over all situations—including yours. Paul called Him "the head over all things" (*Ephesians 1:22, KJV*). How many things? *All* things! Marital issues, financial issues, health-related issues… He is the head over all things. He is the Master!

God says in His Word that He has set Christ Jesus at His own right hand:

Far above all principality, and power, and might, and dominion, and every name that is named, not only in this world, but also in that which is to come: and hath put all things under his feet, and gave him to be the head over all things to the church…

Ephesians 1:21-22, KJV

God has put all things under Jesus' feet. Think about that for a minute. Do you have some knotty problems that are giving you nightmares? They are part of the "all things" that are under the feet of the Master. Do you have some evil forces troubling your life and putting you on the run? They are part of the "all things". "All things" means *all* things—not *some* things. So, you can be assured that there is a Master greater than that troublesome master lording it over you.

Death took Lazarus as its captive, but Christ's response was, "I am the resurrection and the life" (*John 11:25*). In essence, Jesus was saying, "I am the real Master. It is not the devil. It is not death. It is I; I am the real Master."

He Calls for You

"The Master is come, and *calleth for thee*" (*John 11:28, KJV*). One major obstacle that often stands in the way—even when the Master shows up and is ready to bring Lazarus out of the tomb—is our unwillingness to give Him our attention. *He needs our attention.*

Mary had been mourning for the past four days. She was so overwhelmed with her problem that she didn't even notice that the Master had come. Likewise, we are often so broken and battered that we become oblivious of the Lord's presence. Our focus is so much on the issue at hand that we lose sight of the One who has come to give us His solution.

Before Jesus can bring out Lazarus, He needs to get your attention. You must come out of that place of mourning, complaints, regrets, bitterness and self-pity, and give Him your full attention. It is not enough for Him to come; He must have your attention and cooperation. That's how it works.

When God wanted to get Moses out of the wilderness, He sought his attention. He called to him from within the burning bush: "Moses! Moses!" And Moses said, "Here I am" (*Exodus 3:4*). When God wanted to end Sarah's barrenness, He sought her attention. He asked Abraham, ""Where is Sarah your wife?" and Abraham replied, "There, in the tent" (*Genesis 18:9*).

Sarah was probably in the tent, focusing on her problem. She could have been saying to herself, "I just have a few years left to live on earth. Look at me, I'm really old. I can barely move my body. I wonder if I will ever carry my own child, as God promised. Even if I should conceive now, how am I going to push!"

The Master is here, and He calls for you! It is time to come out of the place of mourning. It is time to run out to meet the Master. There are individuals who have kept Him outside for too long. And, as long as you keep Him waiting outside, Lazarus will remain in the grave. The problem will continue to linger.

Why is it so important for the Lord to have our attention? Firstly, because God wants us to be excited over Him:

> And you shall rejoice before the LORD your God, you and your sons and your daughters, your male and female servants, and the Levite who is within your gates…
>
> *Deuteronomy 12:12, NKJV*

> Draw me, we will run after thee: the king hath brought me into his chambers: we will be glad and rejoice in thee, we will remember thy love more than wine: the upright love thee.
>
> *Song of Solomon 1:4, KJV*

God doesn't want you to stay in your tent, complaining and sorrowing. He wants you to come outside and meet Him, rejoicing that He is present and able to get Lazarus out of the tomb. He wants you to recognize His presence and consciously respond to it. The more we keep the Lord waiting, the more we prolong the problem.

Oftentimes the Lord shows up and many of us are not interested in rejoicing over Him. We hear a sermon about God and we say, "I've heard that before." God gives us a word of hope, a word of life, and we say, "I know that." Sometimes, I look at people's attitude during praise and worship and when the Word is preached in church, and I wonder why they bothered to come into God's presence in the first place. No excitement, no life, nothing! Their minds are on the issues back at home. It is time to get up and run into His arms, rejoicing in anticipation of what He is about to do!

Secondly, He needs your attention because He wants you to hear what He has to say. God doesn't just want you to come out of that place of sorrowing merely to rejoice at His feet, He also wants you to hear the good news He has for you.

> And they said to him, Where is Sarah your wife? And he said, [She is here] in the tent.
>
> [The Lord] said, I will surely return to you when the season comes round, and behold, Sarah your wife will have a son. And Sarah was listening and heard it at the tent door which was behind Him.
>
> *Genesis 18:9-10, AMPC*

There are things God wants you to hear before He brings your Lazarus out of the tomb, so He needs your attention.

He may have some instructions for you. You can't hear what He has to say until you give Him your attention. You can't hear what He has to say to you until you quit mourning over Lazarus and run to Him.

Martha, by reason of running to the Lord, had already heard those glorious words of His. She met Jesus with bitterness in her heart but, after her conversation with Him, she had become hopeful that Lazarus would return. Mary also needed that message of hope from the Lord. She needed to stop thinking, "Well, one day when this life is over, all my problems will go away." She needed to hear the good news that the Master could still bring Lazarus to life before the resurrection of the dead.

Until we hear from the Lord, we will believe the lies that the devil has told us. Until we hear from the Lord, we will have a wrong perspective about the problems in our lives. That is why David declared, "How sweet are your words to my taste, sweeter than honey to my mouth!" (*Psalm 119:103*). Thus, he rejoiced at the word of the Lord, like one who finds great treasure (*Psalm 119:162*).

Exposure to God's Word will not only lift your faith, it will also bring sweetness into your life. It puts you in a celebratory mood even before the miracle arrives. This is one of the keys to having your Lazarus back.

4

It's Time to Arise

[She] called Mary her sister secretly, saying, The Master is come, and calleth for thee. As soon as she heard that, she arose quickly, and came unto him.

John 11:29, KJV

For four days, Mary had been sitting and mourning. She had been musing over the good times they had had with Lazarus and the emptiness that his departure would leave in their hearts. But suddenly Martha came and gave her some good news: "The Lord is around, and He wants to see you." Immediately Mary received this message, she got up from the place of mourning. It was time to arise.

She didn't contemplate whether to go or not; "she arose quickly". She didn't say to Martha, "Is He coming only now? What's the point? What is He coming to do, when the deed has already been done?" No, "she arose quickly". There are people who were sitting at the Lord's feet and enjoying the good sermons until they lost Lazarus. After that, they never answered the Lord's call anymore. The Lord has sent for them over and over, but they always sit tight where they are.

After years of following the Lord and sitting at His feet, Mary knew the importance of giving heed to a message from Him. She had come to realize that an invitation from the Lord can mark a turning point in one's life. Bartimaeus was a helpless, blind man until Jesus sent for him. The moment he heard the message, "Be of good cheer. Rise, He is calling you" (*Mark 10:49, NKJV*), he threw aside his garment and made his way into the Lord's presence. His response to the Lord's invitation marked the end of his sorrow and blindness.

Have you ever wondered why many have remained in the same spot, unable to get over certain bad moments? It is the refusal to arise. You can only experience the glory and the light of the Lord when you decide to arise. God is saying to you:

> "Arise, shine, for your light has come, and the glory of the LORD rises upon you. See, darkness covers the earth and thick darkness is over the peoples, but the LORD rises upon you and his glory appears over you.
>
> *Isaiah 60:1-2*

For you to shine, you must arise. For God's glory to rise upon you, you must arise. For you to escape the gross darkness of the devil, you must arise—like the Prodigal Son who, after he got into trouble, resolved, "I will arise and go to my father..." (*Luke 15:18, NKJV*).

Quite often, we see people who arise, only to go into the arms of prostitutes. Some arise and go into old relationships that they had come out of. Others arise and go into drugs or alcohol, hoping that would lift their burdens. And there are also people who arise and turn to false prophets or occultists for solutions. But Mary arose and went straight to the Father. If she had gone somewhere else, Lazarus would never have made it out of the grave. If the Prodigal Son had gone somewhere else, he wouldn't have enjoyed restoration.

Not What You Think

> When the Jews who had been with Mary in the house, comforting her, noticed how quickly she got up and went out, they followed her, supposing she was going to the tomb to mourn there.
>
> *John 11:31*

Gross darkness had covered Mary so much that, each time she left the room, her destination would be the tomb of Lazarus. The devil was always taking her to the grave to remind her of her loss. Each time she went to the tomb, she would recall how she and her sister had sent for Jesus to come and heal Lazarus... but Jesus had failed to show up.

She had been going to the grave to weep. Her movements had become so predictable that, when she went out that day, the Jews thought she was going to embark on one of those mourning trips: "they followed her, supposing she was going to the tomb to mourn there". But this time was different; she wasn't going to mourn at the grave any more.

Like Mary, many of us need to stop revisiting our graves: the graves of past failures, past disappointments, failed relationships, sins already confessed and forgiven by God. Many keep going to those graves until they become so miserable that they can't make any headway in life: "If only that man hadn't jilted me, I would have gone far in life... If I hadn't made that mistake, things would have been better... If I had gone to school like others, my life would have amounted to something... *If...*"

Paul was a man who had many graves to visit. He was part of the team that killed Stephen, one of the finest and most promising disciples of the early church. But Paul had just one thing in mind: "forgetting those things which are behind and reaching forward to those things which are ahead…" (*Philippians 3:13, NKJV*). He refused to make a habit of visiting the grave. There were better things ahead for him, and it was pointless returning to the graves of the past.

It's time you changed your disposition too. The Jews thought Mary was going to sing the same old song and roll on the ground at the tomb, but they were in for a surprise. Her light had come. She was about to receive the oil of joy in place of her mourning. Her focus had to change from the grave to the Lord. When you realize that Christ comes with the oil of joy to replace your mourning, your disposition will change; for He has said:

> "The Spirit of the Lord is upon me; he has appointed me to preach Good News to the poor; he has sent me to heal the brokenhearted…"
>
> *Luke 4:18, TLB*

> He has sent me… to bestow on them a crown of beauty instead of ashes, the oil of joy instead of mourning, and a garment of praise instead of a spirit of despair. They will be called oaks of righteousness, a planting of the Lord for the display of his splendor.
>
> *Isaiah 61:1,3, NIV*

Today, Jesus is on a mission to do the same for you. Arise. Rise up from the place of whining and grumbling over the loss of Lazarus and begin to say, like Habakkuk:

> Though the fig tree does not bud and there are no grapes on the vines, though the olive crop fails and the fields produce no food, though there are no sheep in the pen and no cattle in the stalls, yet I will rejoice in the LORD, I will be joyful in God my Savior.

> The Sovereign LORD is my strength; he makes my feet like the feet of a deer, he enables me to tread on the heights.
>
> *Habakkuk 3:17-19*

If you have complaints and grievances against the Lord, rather than reject His invitation, go to Him and reason it out with Him. Mary did just that; she said, "Lord, if you had been here, my brother would not have died" (*John 11:32*). Notice that the Lord did not rebuke her; in fact, God even invites us to do likewise: "Come now, and let us reason together" (*Isaiah 1:18, KJV*). As it turned out, Mary's "reasoning together" with Jesus resulted in the restoration of Lazarus.

The Urgency of His Call

> As soon as she heard that, she arose quickly, and came unto him.
>
> *John 11:29, KJV*

Notice how the Bible puts it: "she arose quickly". There was urgency in her action. No time to contemplate. No time to argue. No time to consult with those around, to see if it was proper to go or not. *She arose quickly.* That's how God wants us to treat every message and call from Him. To have Lazarus back, you need to respond quickly to the Master. You need to take Him seriously, whatever He demands of you.

Sometimes, when you give people a message from God and you expect them to make a quick decision, they tell you instead, "Well, I will think about it." Sadly, Satan is so ruthless that sometimes he doesn't even give them the chance to think about it. When Felix heard Paul's message about righteousness, temperance, and the judgment to come, he trembled. But, instead of making a decision that would have given him eternal life, he told Paul, "That's enough for now! You may leave. When I find it convenient, I will send for you" (*Acts 24:25*).

The King's matters require urgency. Many are fond of keeping the Lord on their waiting list. God knocks on the door of every heart (*Revelation 3:18*) and, instead of opening immediately, they tell Him, "Hold on a little." But God is not going to hold on forever. He has said, "My Spirit shall not strive with man forever" (*Genesis 6:3, NKJV*).

Only those who are quick to respond to God's message will have a quick solution to their problems. The more you keep Him waiting, the more you keep Lazarus in the grave. Christ's message to Mary was like fire in her bones; she couldn't sit down for another second.

Jeremiah had gone through a season of discouragement and folded up his ministry. But then the Word of the Lord came to him, as it did to Mary: "... his word is in my heart like a fire, a fire shut up in my bones. I am weary of holding it in; indeed, I cannot" (*Jeremiah 20:9*). So, he got up and acted upon God's Word.

We don't seem to have many people like Jeremiah and Mary today. Instead, we have people who are indifferent to God's messages. His Word hardly moves them. They hear sermons on holiness but, after the service, they are back to a life of sin. They hear messages on love, but they will never forgive anyone who hurts them. Paul described them as those "whose consciences have been seared as with a hot iron" (*1 Timothy 4:2*). Such people may spend years in the church but, as long as they are not ready to respond swiftly to God's message, their lives will remain the same.

Why does God's Word require a quick response? Because "the word of God is quick, and powerful" (*Hebrews 4:12, KJV*). A moment's delay can cost you the blessing of a lifetime. It was only a moment's delay that cost Esau his blessing (*Genesis 27:30-38*).

Many women would have been married long ago if only they had heeded God's word and, like Mary, "arose quickly". When God told them, "that's your husband", they argued with Him. "I am going to keep praying about it," they said. "I need to study him more. He doesn't look like a man who can take care of me." Ten years down the line, they are on their knees, crying out to God, "Change my story, Lord." Others have missed out on contracts, on business and ministerial opportunities, because they failed to "arise quickly".

The angel of the Lord told Philip, "Arise and go toward the south along the road which goes down from Jerusalem to Gaza" (*Acts 8:26, NKJV*). So, Philip promptly "arose and went" (*Acts 8:27, NKJV*). If he had waited till the next day, he would have missed the opportunity to win the Ethiopian eunuch to Christ (*Acts 8:27-38*). The next task that God had for Philip was also urgent—so urgent, in fact, that the Holy Spirit had to transport him quickly on His wings to Azotus (*Acts 8:39-40*).

Jesus said, "I must work the works of Him who sent Me while it is day; the night is coming when no one can work" (*John 9:4, NKJV*). He had three years as His "day". What if He had wasted those three years that God had earmarked for His work? The moment the Spirit came upon Him in the River Jordan, He arose quickly.

Quit striving with the Lord. Quit arguing with Him. Rise up quickly, and God will bring your Lazarus back to life.

5

The Character of Christ

Therefore, when Jesus saw her weeping, and the Jews who came with her weeping, He groaned in the spirit and was troubled. And He said, "Where have you laid him?"

They said to Him, "Lord, come and see."

Jesus wept.

John 11:33-35, NKJV

The passage above reveals a portrait of Christ that is worth looking at, because it will enable us to relate better with Him as we look forward to the restoration of our Lazarus.

Before coming to Bethany, Jesus had the assurance that Lazarus would come back to life (*John 11:4-14*). But, despite this foreknowledge, He was brought to tears when He arrived at the scene of the tragedy. What did the Lord see that He couldn't help but weep?

He saw the cruelty of the devil, the thief that comes to steal, kill and destroy. He saw the victims of this cruel oppressor who had resolved that "I will pursue, I will overtake them... I will gorge myself on them... my hand will destroy them" (*Exodus 15:9*). He wept because He saw the people's utter helplessness in the face of the devil's onslaught. Once the enemy struck Lazarus, it was a futile battle on Mary and Martha's part to keep their brother alive.

It was easy, without the Lord's intervention, for the devil to bring untold grief and hardship to this once-happy family. But it wasn't just about them. Yes, the anguish of this bereaved family and their community was immense; but it was nothing compared to the torment of millions in the pit of hell, taken as eternal captives by the devil. It was therefore impossible for the Lord not to weep. It was an act prompted by His grief for the suffering of humanity.

Christ's weeping here touches on His very nature and the nature of the Father, which is love, pity and compassion. In his admonition to the Jews who were going through trials and suffering, James made this important remark:

> You have heard of the perseverance of Job and seen the end intended by the Lord—that the Lord is very compassionate and merciful.
>
> *James 5:11, NKJV*

I want you to take note of how James described the Lord: "very compassionate". The Lord isn't just compassionate; He is *very* compassionate. He is compassionate towards us when the storms of life hit us: "As a father has compassion on his children, so the LORD has compassion on those who fear him" (*Psalm 103:13*).

It is important that we approach the Lord with this mindset. To have your Lazarus back, you will need someone who feels the very emotions that run through your soul. Sometimes, people say to us, "I know how you feel." But do they? They may be genuinely concerned about me, but it will be difficult for them to know exactly how I feel. When I lost my father, there was a moment at the hospital when I felt an emotion that was beyond words. Amidst tears, I muttered to no one in particular, "How am I going to go through this?" Only the Lord knows how we feel at such points in our life; and that's why He is the most qualified person to step into the situation and help us out.

The Advocate Who Never Lost a Case

> And Jesus lifted up His eyes and said, "Father, I thank You that You have heard Me. And I know that You always hear Me, but because of the people who are standing by I said this, that they may believe that You sent Me."
>
> *John 11:41-42*

Jesus said, "I know that You always hear Me." Why was He always getting a positive response from the Father? It was partly because of His ability to convey our emotions to the Father. When Christ stands before Him to plead our case, the Father can feel the very emotions that we feel. Jesus doesn't just take our case to the Father; He equally takes our feelings to Him. Mike Murdock, in his book *The Leadership Secrets of Jesus*, told an interesting story which illustrates this point. I will share it below, in my own words.

There was once a renowned lawyer who won just about every case he took on and always managed to secure million-dollar settlements for his clients. He had a protégé, a young lawyer, who became puzzled as to how his mentor did it. It wasn't in the research or in the documents submitted to court, which were all nothing out of the ordinary. But, whenever the great lawyer presented his case before the jury, they would be so moved that they would give his client enormous settlements.

Baffled, the young lawyer asked his mentor what his secret was. The old man replied, "It's quite simple really, but you will not believe me even if I were to tell you." The young man, however, refused to be put off and continued to ply his mentor with questions. Finally, one day, the great lawyer invited him to go for a drive with him. First, they stopped at a grocery store, where the old man loaded his car with groceries; then they drove out into the country. Snow had been falling heavily for several days, and it was bitterly cold. At last they drove up to a small farmhouse, where the lawyer told his protégé to help him carry in the groceries.

In the house was a little boy who had both his legs cut off; he had lost them in a car accident. The old lawyer spoke with the boy's parents for some time and then said, "Just thought I'd drop by with a few groceries, since it must be hard for you to get out in this freezing weather."

On the drive back, the old lawyer said, "I win my cases because I really do care about my clients; it's that simple. I feel they deserve the best settlement possible and, when I present my case to the jury, they feel it too. They return the verdicts I want. I go into court, feeling what my clients feel. And the court begins to feel what I feel."

The Father hears Jesus always, because Jesus doesn't just approach Him with your requests; He approaches Him with your feelings, and the Father is very mindful of your feelings. God said something profound to Moses to let him know the rationale behind his rescue mission to Egypt:

"I have surely seen the oppression of My people who are in Egypt, and have heard their cry because of their taskmasters, for I know their sorrows."

Exodus 3:7, NKJV

Look at the last part of that verse: "I know their sorrows." It is encouraging to know that "He knows". Eli, even with his *priestly* eyes, mistook Hannah's moving lips for a sign that she was drunk, but the one who knows our sorrows saw that she was in deep anguish (*1 Samuel 1:10*).

There is an increasing level of aloofness and selfishness in the world and even in the church today. This is a deviation from the nature of God. Sometimes I hear people narrate tragic incidents that happened to others, and you can't feel any tinge of pain in their voice. So long as they are not the victim, it's alright. In this era of smart phones with cameras, it is common to see people snapping away, taking pictures of accident victims rather than offering them help. People are more interested in recording and narrating the painful situations of their neighbours than in stepping forward to give a helping hand. Why? Because they don't *know* the sorrow of those involved; there's an emotional detachment.

Once I was editing a report on the funeral service of an elderly man, and I was shocked at the way our cameraman took his time to record the corpse. The images he captured were disturbing and I wondered, how was it possible for him to focus on the dead body and film it so nonchalantly? Then I realized, it was because he didn't *know* the sorrow of those who were bereaved. He could look at that body without batting an eyelid, but those who knew the sorrow would have found it unbearable to record or watch those clips.

After the burial of my father, I never bothered to ask for the recording of the funeral. I never bothered to ask for the pictures. I was not interested in them, either for record purposes or as a reminder. Why? Because *I know the sorrow.*

Jesus Wept

Let's take a closer look at how the Lord *knowing their sorrow* contributed to the resurrection of Lazarus. The Bible says "Jesus wept." He wasn't just sad; He groaned and He wept. A whole verse was dedicated to those two words—Jesus wept. It wasn't a light shedding of tears. It was a deep outpouring of sorrow that needed to stand alone as a verse. It tells a whole lot about the Lord and why it is His deepest desire to give you back your Lazarus.

Firstly, He wept because He considered the victims as His own brothers and sisters:

> Both Jesus who sanctifies and those who are sanctified... are all from one Father; for this reason He is not ashamed to call them brothers and sisters...
>
> *Hebrews 2:11, AMP*

Jesus didn't just consider the death of Lazarus as the death of Mary and Martha's brother; He considered it as the death of *His* own brother—the one He loved. It was therefore impossible for Him to walk around with a sense of coldness. He had lost a brother: "the one you love" (*John 11:3*). Do you see Jesus like that? Do you know that Jesus considers you as His brother... as His sister?

You think He isn't bothered, because He isn't the one "the thing happened to"? Change your thinking about the Lord! The Bible says that He calls us "brothers and sisters". When you lose that job, He says, "My brother has lost his job. I can feel his pain." When you are betrayed, He says, "My sister has been betrayed. I have been betrayed too, so I know how it feels."

After His resurrection, Jesus told Mary Magdalene to "go to My brethren and say to them, 'I am ascending to My Father and your Father...'" (*John 20:17, NKJV*). "My brethren"—that's you and me. We, together with Jesus, are children of the same Father, for He said, "I am ascending to My Father and your Father..." He is our elder brother:

> For those God foreknew he also predestined to be conformed to the image of his Son, that he might be the firstborn among many brothers and sisters.
>
> *Romans 8:29*

You have an elder brother in Christ. Think of what your earthly brothers can do for you; the lengths they will go to, just to meet your needs and keep you happy. You have an even better brother in Christ Jesus. He is not ashamed to call you "brother". He is not ashamed to call you "sister". When you smile, He is happy. And when you weep, He weeps with you.

Praise God that we are Christ's many brethren in God's family (*Ephesians 3:15*). That's why it is easy for Him to share in our sorrows and intervene on our behalf. The writer of Hebrews says, "Therefore, in all things He had to be made like His brethren, that He might be a merciful and faithful High Priest..." Take note of this— "*all things*". It includes your present situation.

Our Pastor

> He tends his flock like a shepherd: he gathers the lambs in his arms and carries them close to his heart; he gently leads those that have young.
>
> *Isaiah 40:11*

Jesus was and is our Pastor. He says to us, "I am the good Shepherd" (*John 10:11*). "Shepherd" is another word for Pastor. Peter called Him "the Shepherd and Overseer of your souls" (*1 Peter 2:25*) and "the Chief Shepherd" (*1 Peter 5:4*).

It was easy for Jesus, as the Pastor of Mary, Martha, to weep—because He had a shared feeling with the weaknesses of His sheep. I have seen church members who quit going to church because their pastors had no shared feeling with their weaknesses. A friend once told me how his pastor threatened to deal with him "personally" after he fell into sin. While this young man was seeking for restoration and battling with guilt, his pastor was more interested in dealing with him "personally". No shared feeling.

But look at Mary and Martha's Pastor: "he gathers the lambs in his arms and carries them close to his heart". He can feel their emotions and their pain because they are right in His arms, close to His heart. He "gently leads those that have young". Those that have young are those with burdens, some additional cares to worry about—just like Mary and Martha. We have this assurance from the Word of God:

> For we do not have a High Priest Who is unable to understand and sympathize and have a shared feeling with our weaknesses and infirmities and liability to the assaults of temptation, but One Who has been tempted in every respect as we are, yet without sinning.
>
> *Hebrews 4:15, AMPC*

He treats us based on this "shared feeling". He empathizes with us and wades into our situations because He understands. Look at what is mentioned: "our weaknesses and infirmities and liability to the assaults of temptation".

People hardly understand our liability to temptation. That's why many times you hear them say, "How could brother so-and-so do a thing like that!" Many would have queried Peter's loyalty to the Lord when he denied Him: "I thought brother Peter was genuinely born again. I didn't know it was just eye-service. You can't trust anybody!" But his Pastor understood. He knew his "liability to the assaults of temptation" and so, when Peter eventually fell, the Lord didn't tell him, "I will personally deal with you."

The Lord said, ""I am the good shepherd; I know my sheep" (*John 10:14*). Their weaknesses, their infirmities, their liability to the assaults of temptation—these are just a few of the things He knows. Mary and Martha knew this, so it was very easy for them to run to Him the moment they heard He was coming. In fact, Mary met Him outside the town (*John 11:30*). She did what the writer of Hebrews advised:

> Let us then fearlessly and confidently and boldly draw near to the throne of grace (the throne of God's unmerited favour to us sinners), that we may receive mercy [for our failures] and find grace to help in good time for every need [appropriate help and well-timed help, coming just when we need it].
>
> *Hebrews 4:16, AMPC*

She went confidently and boldly before the Lord—and "appropriate help and well-timed help" came, just when she needed it. You too will find help when you run confidently to Pastor Jesus with your "weaknesses and infirmities and liability to the assaults of temptation".

A Shared Feeling

The ministry of Christ contains many instances of the Lord meeting the needs of His sheep because of this "shared feeling". The Gospel of Matthew relates how, when He saw the multitudes of people, "He was moved with compassion for them, because they were weary and scattered, like sheep having no shepherd" (*Matthew 9:36, NKJV*). Further along, we read about how He came across another great multitude and "was moved with compassion for them, and healed their sick" (*Matthew 14:14, NKJV*).

Then, in the next chapter, we see Him feeding yet another multitude (four thousand men, besides women and children) after multiplying seven loaves of bread and a few fishes. This miracle was not meant to prove to the people that He was Almighty God; it was because He understood the people's predicament—a shared feeling. He said:

> "I have compassion on the multitude, because they have now continued with Me three days and have nothing to eat. And I do not want to send them away hungry, lest they faint on the way."
>
> *Matthew 15:32, NKJV*

You see, Jesus wasn't only concerned about the people's present hunger; He was equally concerned about the resultant effect—the people fainting on the way. Jesus doesn't just think about our present circumstances; He also looks at the problems we could encounter later in life. Sometimes we say, "Oh, if things go on like this, my future will be terrible. I don't know what will become of me." He's aware of that future, and He has plans for you.

All He requires is that you continue with Him: "they have now continued with Me three days." He wants you to do the same. Don't run away. Don't say, "If I continue with Him, I will die of hunger in this wilderness." No, He has plans to provide abundantly for you. He made sure that there was more than enough for the people to eat—and even to bring home to their families too! Even after those hungry people had eaten two or three rounds, there were still "seven large baskets" (*Matthew 15:37, NKJV*) full of the food that was left over. Those who had left Him the first and second day couldn't partake of this great blessing. It pays to continue with Him.

Mary and Martha continued with Him. After four days, He eventually stepped in. He is stepping into your problem right now. He is bringing you out of that mess right now. He is coming with the reward of continuing with Him after four days of having Lazarus in the grave and three days of staying at His feet without food: "So do not throw away your confidence; it will be richly rewarded" (*Hebrews 10:36*).

A Glimpse of His Love

The Jews said, See how [tenderly] He loved him!

John 11:36, AMPC

For once, the focus of the people shifted from death and mourning to the Lord. They caught a glimpse of His heart, and they could only exclaim, "How tenderly He loved him!" Their doubts ended. Their arguments about Christ not loving His friend enough to run down to Bethany when He heard of his illness ceased. It was now crystal clear that Jesus truly loved Lazarus.

It is this same picture that the Lord wants His children to see; His desire is for us to get into the well of His heart and see the depth of His love for us. When Paul bowed his knees to pray for the church at Ephesus, he wanted them to see what those Jews, those neighbours of Mary and Martha, saw—and even more. He said, "For this reason I kneel before the Father…" (*Ephesians 2:14*). He wasn't kneeling to pray for them to acquire more houses and buy more cars. He wanted God to grant them, among other things, the ability to "comprehend with all saints what is the breadth, and length, and depth, and height" of Christ's love for them, and "to know the love of Christ, which passes knowledge…" (*Ephesians 3:18-19, AKJV*).

We should pray for God to do same for us: that we really come to "know [practically, through experience]" for ourselves "the love of Christ, which far surpasses mere knowledge" (*Ephesians 3:19, AMPC*). The Jews had only a glimpse of it. Even Mary and Martha had just a glimpse of it; it was only when Jesus went to the cross that they saw a greater dimension of it.

Are you feeling like Mary and Martha at the tomb of Lazarus? Pray and ask the Father to reveal to you this love of Christ that surpasses knowledge. Paul had a rough life, with Satan buffeting him everywhere he went. What did God do for him? He showed him a picture of Christ's love and Paul began to ask:

Who shall separate us from the love of Christ? Shall tribulation, or distress, or persecution, or famine, or nakedness, or peril, or sword?

Romans 8:35, NKJV

The revelation of Christ's love brought Paul to the point of conviction, and he penned down this powerful statement:

> For I am persuaded that neither death nor life, nor angels nor principalities nor powers, nor things present nor things to come, nor height nor depth, nor any other created thing, shall be able to separate us from the love of God which is in Christ Jesus our Lord.
>
> *Romans 8:38-39, NKJV*

Take some time off and ask God to reveal to you His love which is in Christ Jesus. It will not only help you in your walk with the Lord, it will also be crucial in getting back your Lazarus. The Jews said, "See how tenderly He loved him!" The same can be said of His love for you—*see how tenderly He loves you!* I bow my knees and pray that, even this very moment, you will receive a revelation of Christ's immeasurable love for you. Amen.

6

Dealing with the Grave

And He said, Where have you laid him? They said to Him, Lord, come and see.

John 11:34, AMPC

When Jesus was set to bring Lazarus back to life, He asked, "Where have you laid him?" He wanted to be taken to his grave. Before you can have your Lazarus back, Christ needs to deal with *the power of the grave.* Lazarus couldn't come back to life until Jesus had dealt with the power of the grave.

In this chapter, I will show you what the grave is about and how its power affects our lives. Let me also state here, that you don't have to be physically dead to be under attack from the power of the grave or under its influence; many who are physically alive today are suffering under its power.

To understand *the power of the grave* and why Christ had to deal with it, we shall look at what the grave signifies.

Finality

But the dead know nothing; they don't even have their memories. Whatever they did in their lifetimes—loving, hating, envying—is long gone, and they have no part in anything here on earth anymore.

Ecclesiastes 9:5b-6, TLB

The grave speaks of finality. It is the physical emblem of a journey that has come to an end; a final reminder of a story that is over. It is this sense of finality that causes people to grieve inconsolably when a body is lowered into the grave. Why? Because, once the body goes down to the grave, all hope of ever seeing the dead person again vanishes.

Every day we read of couples getting divorced because of what is often described as "irreconcilable differences". The Oxford Dictionary puts it this way: "If differences or disagreements are irreconcilable, they are so great that it is not possible to settle them." Such a union is dead. I have witnessed such cases, where not even the efforts of pastors, relatives or friends could change the story. The couples went ahead to start new relationships. Why? Because the marriage came under the attack of *the power of the grave.* Whenever the power of the grave attacks a union, it leaves a mark of finality.

Do your relationships keep ending irreconcilably? It is the power of the grave at work. You need to take Jesus to the graveyard of your relationships; like Mary and Martha, you need to tell Him, "Lord, come and see."

We see a classic example of this in *John 4:4-42,* which tells the story of how Jesus met the Samaritan woman at the well. In the course of their discussion together, the Lord told her, ""Go, call your husband and come back" (*John 4:16*). She answered, "I have no husband." Jesus then said to her, "The fact is, you have had five husbands, and the man you now have is not your husband" (*John 4:18*).

What happened after the first marriage? The power of the grave struck, and there was no way the relationship could stay alive. The second husband came and the same power struck, leaving a mark of finality. It went on till she had had five husbands and finally decided, "I'll just have to forget about this marriage thing. Let me find a man I can stay with, with no strings attached." The power of the grave had wearied her.

We find this power of "finality" at work in health-related issues too. Often, we hear of someone having a "terminal" condition—meaning the illness or disease is incurable and will lead to the person's death. A typical example is AIDS. The power of the grave is at work here, attacking its prey with the aim of dealing a final blow to it.

The Bible tells us, "Elisha had become sick with the illness of which he would die" (*2 Kings 13:14, NKJV*). It wasn't just some sickness; it was one that came with the spirit of finality; it was the power of the grave.

Paul, too, would have lost one of his fellow soldiers—Epaphroditus—to this power of finality, but for God's intervention: "For indeed he was sick almost unto death; but God had mercy on him..." (*Philippians 2:27, NKJV*). It was the power of the grave that wanted to cut short the life and work of this man; but God saved him.

The power of the grave might be after your business, your career, your relationships, or even your family. But we have a God who can quench its fiery fire.

"I am the Omega"

I am the Alpha and the Omega, *the Beginning and the End*, says the Lord God, He Who is and Who was and Who is to come, the Almighty (the Ruler of all).

Revelation 1:8, AMPC

> I am the Alpha and the Omega, the First and the Last...
>
> *Revelation 1:11, AMPC*

> Do not be afraid! I am the First and the Last...
>
> *Revelation 1:17, AMPC*

In these Scriptures, we find the answer to the grave's power of finality. Jesus said, "I am the Omega... the End... the Last... the Almighty." What all this implies is that He has the last word, the final say. He possesses the Power of Finality to end all powers of finality. Without such a Power stepping up to the grave, Lazarus would have remained under the grip of death. That same Power is intervening in your life right now; it is addressing every ailment and every problem that bears a sting of finality.

It took Omega to bring Lazarus back from the grave. It takes the One whose name is Omega to reverse the sentence of the grave when you see your marriage heading towards the point of "irreconcilable differences". It takes the One who is Omega to reverse the doctors' diagnosis when they pronounce your ailment as "terminal". It takes Omega to reverse the power of finality over your business, your career, your relationships and your family.

Someone greater is on your side: the Omega; the One who put an end to the suffering of the woman with the issue of blood; who changed the story of the woman at the well, from being a serial divorcee to the beloved daughter of her community. There is indeed Someone greater, who is working in your favour this very moment—JESUS, the King of Glory; the OMEGA. Just say to Him, "Lord, come and see," and He will take care of the rest.

A Mask

> You are like whitewashed tombs, which look beautiful on the outside but on the inside are full of the bones of the dead and everything unclean.
>
> *Matthew 23:27*

The grave serves as a mask. Jesus described it as appearing beautiful outwardly, but full of dead bones and uncleanness within. Have you seen people whose lives are like that? Everything looks beautiful on the outside. You may even envy them and wish to be like them. They look like they have it all but, on the inside, they are full of dead bones. On the inside, they are full of bitterness, carrying memories of childhood abuse, betrayal, fears and stinging remarks that seem indelible.

These people may wear nice clothes, have good jobs, and present a smiling face to the world; but inside, they are like dead bones. That's a grave life they are living. Jesus described the graves as "beautiful": white, innocuous and decorated with lovely flowers. But hidden inside are horrors that would make you cringe if you could only see them.

We have seen "normal" people committing suicide for no good reason. They weren't looking sad on the outside; but inside were dead bones that were eating them up. They had issues and problems that made them hate this life. On 19 March 2017, a medical doctor in my country was returning home from church when he suddenly stopped on a bridge and jumped into the lagoon below. The deceased had taken the car keys from his driver and driven a few meters before jumping into the lagoon. In a country with a high level of unemployment, this young man had a good job, a car and a driver. But even though everything looked perfect on the outside, he had deep-seated problems eating him up on the inside. That was a life under attack by *the power of the grave.*

Are you living a grave life? Are you hiding dead things inside that no one knows about? Jesus is saying, "Take me to where you laid him." He wants to address that grave life and make you beautiful, not only on the outside, but inside as well. Say to Him, as Mary and Martha did, "Lord, come and see".

The second aspect of this grave life which Christ is interested in dealing with is the mask of uncleanness. The Pharisees were a perfect example of this. On the outside, they appeared righteous to all men, but inside they were "full of hypocrisy and wickedness" (*Matthew 23:28*). People with a grave life may sing in the choir and look glorious to the congregation; but fornication, malice and gossip are part of their daily lives. They may be on the prayer team and speak in tongues; but they beat up their wives and have extramarital affairs. They may be called deacons in church; but in their offices and places of work they live like vipers. They have a dual personality, just like the grave. You may see the outside but not the inner man.

Matthew chapter 23 contains one of Christ's most fiery messages, and it was targeted at people with a grave life: people who speak in tongues in church and return home to watch pornography; people who smile at everyone but are full of wickedness and envy on the inside. They look impressive on the outside but, on the inside, they are full of dead bones and filth.

Jesus wants to do something about that grave. He said to Mary and Martha, "Where have you laid him?" Are you willing to take Jesus to your grave? Are you willing to let Him do a surgical operation on your life, so that both the inside and the outside can become a pleasing sight to the Father? If you are, go ahead and say to Him, "Lord, come and see."

Education can change our thinking, but it cannot change our spirit man. That is why we still have professors and CEOs who cheat on their spouses. Only Christ can do something about the dead bones and filth in the spirit and soul.

Plastic surgery can change one's external appearance, but it can't change what's inside. A beauty makeover on the outside won't necessarily transform the ugly nature within. Only Christ can do something about the inside.

Jesus gave a perfect picture of a grave-like church in *Revelation 3:14-20*. This church seemed to be like our ideal church in modern times: it looked rich, had acquired wealth, and did not need a thing. That was the image on the outside. But, on the inside, Jesus saw something different; He saw the dead bones and the filth, and He said, "you are wretched, pitiful, poor, blind and naked" (*Revelation 3:17*). Jesus told them, "Take me to the grave, and I will give you gold refined in the fire, so you can be truly rich; and white clothes to wear, so you can cover your shameful nakedness; and medicine to put on your eyes, so you can see."

Jesus wants to do all that and more, if only we will take Him to the grave. Just go ahead and tell Him, "Lord, come and see."

An Unprofitable Investment

What does God see when He looks at a grave? Quite often, He sees a project that He invested so much in, but never got the desired result. When God took Ezekiel to a mass grave, the prophet saw dry bones; but that wasn't what God saw. God saw "an exceedingly great army" (*Ezekiel 37:10, NKJV*). Those dry bones were generals, majors, colonels and captains, with troops of soldiers under them, and they could take on any enemy.

It has often been said that the graveyard is the richest place on earth. That's where you will find great musicians whose songs were never composed. That's where you will find great writers whose books were never written. That's where you will find great inventors whose works never came into existence.

My concern, however, and God's major concern, is not about the dead; it's about the living. God is concerned about the people who, though they are alive, are living "a grave life". What's a grave life? It's a life that is in sharp contrast to its divine purpose and potential. Every building you see has been designed by an architect, who drew up detailed plans for it; but the design can be messed up. God has a design for your life, but that design can also be messed up.

> In Him we also were made [God's] heritage (portion) and we obtained an inheritance; for we had been foreordained (chosen and appointed beforehand) in accordance with His purpose, Who works out everything in agreement with the counsel and design of His [own] will…
>
> *Ephesians 1:11, AMPC*

Note three key words used here: God's "purpose", "design" and "will". They speak of God's blueprint or masterplan for each one of us. When I walk through certain streets in my country, I see women who, by divine design, are supposed to be wonderful mothers and heads of organizations; but instead they are busy jostling for "customers". Something terrible has happened to them: the devil has tampered with the original design of their lives and turned them into prostitutes.

Go to bar parlours and see those lousy fellows idling away their lives, talking about women and politics. Is that what God has for them in His original masterplan? I really doubt it. And how about those church members busily fighting one another for leadership positions, when God has anointed them to do great exploits? And then there's the choir leader who, by divine design, was anointed to bring down God's presence through worship songs—but has chosen instead to sing about women so that he can become a superstar and win a Grammy. These are all dry bones in a mass grave, and they don't please Jesus one bit.

His aim of going to Bethany was to restore the true Lazarus; to make him a living, productive fellow. Similarly, He wants to bring out the "real you". He doesn't want the grave to keep holding you down, depriving you of all the great things He has invested in your life. He doesn't want you to be wasting away in the arms of Delilah, when the Spirit of God is supposed to be moving you in the Camp of Dan (*Judges 16*). He doesn't want you to waste away in the prison, when you are supposed to be telling Pharaoh and his lords how Egypt should be governed (*Genesis 41:14-44*).

He doesn't want you to languish in the wilderness while God's people wait for you to come and take off Goliath's head (*1 Samuel 17*). No, He wants to deliver you from the power of the grave, so that you can be who He created you to be.

If you aren't satisfied with your present state, then it's an indication that you are living a *grave life*. God wants to get the best out of His investment in our lives. When He invests, He expects a profit. That profit is the output of our life: an output that brings Him glory and equally brings satisfaction to us. Point that grave out to Him and pray, "Lord, come and see".

The Lonely Grave

God has said,

> "Never will I leave you; never will I forsake you."

Hebrews 13:5

Lazarus was left alone in the grave, but Jesus said, "I want to go to where you have laid him."

The grave is a lonely place. It is an emblem of loneliness. There, you won't find your friends or loved ones. Love, companionship, togetherness: all these end at the mouth of the grave. It is a place of desertion. No one, out of love for Lazarus, took his or her belongings to go and stay with him at the grave. In life, there will be times when you will be alone like Lazarus. No one will be by your side in that lonely place—no one except Jesus.

Many today are experiencing this *grave-life*: married women who live with their husbands but, deep inside, they are lonely; children who live with their siblings but, deep inside, they are lonely; pastors who have big congregations but, deep inside, they are lonely. Jesus had twelve disciples but, when He got to Gethsemane, He experienced loneliness.

> "A time is coming and in fact has come when you will be scattered, each to your own home. You will leave me all alone. Yet I am not alone, for my Father is with me."
>
> *John 16:32*

When life brings you to that point of loneliness, say to Jesus, as Mary and Martha did: "Lord, come and see." Others may not be interested in your grave. They may not understand your feelings. They may be too busy for you. At most, they may refer you to a counsellor or psychologist, just so that you don't "die of depression". But the Lord not only stands by us when we are in this lonely grave, He wants to bring us out of it. People around you may be gossiping about how you are always "keeping to yourself" and how miserable you look; but rest assured that His presence is with you and that He will get you out of the grave.

Genesis chapter 29 tells the story of how Jacob ended up marrying two sisters: Leah and Rachel. Jacob loved Rachel and laboured seven years for her hand in marriage; but, when those seven years were up, Laban—the girls' father—gave him Leah instead. It was an act that would make Leah's life and marriage a lonely grave. She didn't have the charm of her younger sister, so she had never caught Jacob's eye. The moment Jacob discovered he had been tricked and given Leah instead of the more beautiful Rachel, the honeymoon came to an abrupt end. One can imagine Jacob telling her, "Look, this marriage isn't my idea;

it was your father's idea. You knew from Day One that you were never the love of my life. Rachel is the woman I want. And, to prove it, I will go after her—even if it means working for your father for another seven years."

Your spouse, fiancé or parents may have ignored you in their quest for "Rachel", but God is going to step in and bring you out of that lonely grave. Leah was trapped in a shell of loneliness, but "the LORD saw that Leah was hated" (*Genesis 29:31, KJV*), and so He enabled her to bear children whilst Rachel remained childless. God can see all the issues that have brought hate and loneliness into your life.

He stepped in and began to bring Leah out of her grave. She had her first child and said, "Surely my husband will love me now" (but he didn't). She had the second one and said, "Because the LORD has heard I was hated, he has therefore given me this son also." She conceived again and said, "Wow, now this time will my husband be joined to me" (again he didn't).

By the time she conceived her fourth child, however, her song had changed from hate and loneliness to praise: "Now will I praise the LORD: therefore, I will call him Judah (meaning 'praise')." God had brought her out of the lonely grave and restored to her all the happiness the devil had taken away from her life and marriage. He can do same for you and me. By the time Jacob saw that God's promise of making him the father of many nations was gradually being fulfilled through Leah, he had no choice but to pay attention to her.

Perhaps you are now in a lonely grave because of the people who have abandoned you. Or perhaps you are there now because the people you trusted have mistreated you.

Perhaps you found yourself in this lonely grave because those who are supposed to care for you are busy with their own affairs and consider you a liability. Or your kids have grown up and stopped visiting—or your spouse has pushed you away to this lonely grave because he is preoccupied with people and projects that he finds more interesting than you. Maybe it was your church that got you into this solitary grave with the way they made you feel unimportant. Or you were on the verge of tying the knot when your fiancé—or fiancée—came up with some flimsy excuse that "both of us aren't compatible". Since then you have been a lonely figure, left alone like Lazarus and feeling sore about it.

Like David, you are probably saying, "I water my couch with my tears" (*Psalm 6:6, KJV*). But it's time to quit the all-night crying; the Lord has finally come to Bethany. He is right in your house, in your office, in your school; He wants to know where the grave is. He wants to bring you out, like He brought Lazarus. It's time to stop thinking you are alone in this dark grave of loneliness. Today, the Lord is saying, "be sure of this—that I am with you always, even to the end of the world" (*Matthew 28:20, TLB*).

"You will never walk alone"

I remember the long bus ride I took to attend my mother-in-law's funeral in January 2017. It was a difficult time, with the recession in the nation biting hard. The last time I travelled to my in-law's village was during my traditional marriage. Then, I had gone with many family members, friends and church members. There were so many people with me that I had all the support I needed.

But, as I travelled back for this funeral, there were just four people with me: my wife, my mother, and my two sons. Others, who had wanted to come, couldn't—largely because of financial challenges.

My family sat in the back seat while I sat in the front, with a hostile and self-centred stranger beside me. As we waited for passengers to fill up the bus, a little boy came to my side and handed me a club sticker with these words on it: *"You will never walk alone."* I read it and knew without a doubt that it was the Lord who had sent this message to me—I wasn't alone. And it proved to be so, as He stood by me and got us out of all the problems we encountered. With Jesus, you will never walk alone!

Paul, too, remembered a period in his life when everyone forsook him: "The first time I was brought before the judge, no one was here to help me. Everyone had run away" (*2 Timothy 4:16, TLB*). But that wasn't the end of the story. Paul went on to say, "But the Lord stood at my side and gave me strength" (*2 Timothy 4:17*).

In fact, Paul often found himself in great danger, but the Lord always stood by him. On one occasion, even the commander of the Roman army was afraid that Paul would be torn to pieces by his enemies; but we are told that "the following night the Lord stood by him and said, 'Be of good cheer, Paul'" (*Acts 23:11, NKJV*). The same Jesus is standing by you in your loneliness and saying, "Be of good cheer."

7

Dealing with the Stone

Jesus said, "Take away the stone."

John 11:39a, NKJV

Jesus finally came to the tomb, but He couldn't do any miracle until the stone at the tomb was removed. It is important to note that it wasn't Jesus who removed the stone. That wasn't His business. So, when you bring Jesus to the grave (the place of your problem), expect to see His mighty power—but be ready to play your part. There were some aspects of the restoration process that He expected Mary and her people to handle. In this case, they were to "take away the stone". Until you take away the stone, Jesus will not make the next move in restoring your Lazarus.

I will touch on some of the "stones" that you are expected to take away before the Lord can issue the final command, "Lazarus, come forth." These stones act as barriers, but you have what it takes to remove them. If God is telling you, "do it", it is because He knows you have the power to do it.

1. Satanic Stones

These stones are evil spirits assigned to your Lazarus. Their task is to ensure that Lazarus stays right there in the grave and rot away. When Jesus died, physical and spiritual guards were assigned to hold Him down in the grave. But they failed at their task because God intervened on the third day:

> God raised Him up, liberating Him from the pangs of death, seeing that it was not possible for Him to continue to be controlled or retained by it.
>
> *Acts 2:24, AMPC*

You see, the spirit of death and other spiritual forces stood at the gate to control and retain Christ. They probably have been doing the same to you, controlling and retaining the blessings you were meant to enjoy. But, at the tomb of Jesus, God got them out of the way with a powerful earthquake and an angel who rolled back the stone—which made those guards so terrified that "they shook and became like dead men" (*Matthew 28:2-4*).

Similarly, evil spirits and their agents—witches, wizards, occultists and other human or physical agents—may even now be acting as stones to block your Lazarus from coming out of the grave. While witches and wizards work through spells, curses, divination and sorcery, these evil spirits back them up by providing the spiritual powers needed for their devilish machinations. Their collaborative work can be likened to that of the horse and his rider in *Exodus 15:1*. These satanic stones can stand in your way, depriving you of the healing, children, husband, success or any other blessing that you desire of the Lord. Paul said of them:

> For we wrestle not against flesh and blood, but against principalities, against powers, against the rulers of the darkness of this world, against spiritual wickedness in high places.
>
> *Ephesians 6:12, KJV*

We wrestle, of course! Not against flesh and blood—physical opponents—but against spiritual forces! We might believe, out of ignorance, that everything is normal. But, no! We are up against evil forces. They would be so glad to control and retain your treasures for as long as you live. These satanic stones, according to *Ephesians 6:12*, include principalities, powers, rulers of the darkness of this world, and spiritual wickedness in high places. You will find, among this list, the stone standing in your way that you will need to remove. But you won't be doing it by means of physical might or intellectual ability. Why? Because God's Word tells us that, "though we walk in the flesh, we do not war according to the flesh" (*2 Corinthians 10:3, NKJV*).

Our problems may be physical, but not all of them have physical roots. So, to gain victory over them, we should quit warring "according to the flesh". Psychology, philosophy and all the other "sophies" of the world can't remove satanic stones. If any of the forces mentioned above is the stone behind your marital problems, fruitlessness or ill-health, then wrestling in the flesh will never give you total victory.

It is against this background that the Lord expects us to "take away" the stone. You may ask, "Why won't the Lord take away the stone for me?" *Ephesians 1:19-23* gives us the answer. After God raised Jesus from the dead, He set Him at His own right hand in the heavenly places (*verse 20*), far above all these stones:

> Far above all rule and authority and power and dominion and every name that is named... not only in this age and in this world, but also in the age and the world which are to come...
>
> *Ephesians 1:21, AMPC*

What is most interesting, however, is the statement made in the next two verses:

> And He has put all things under His feet and has appointed Him the universal and supreme Head of the Church [a headship exercised throughout the Church], which is His body...
>
> *Ephesians 1:22-23, AMPC*

The Church—which includes you and me—is part of Christ's Body. As the Head, He exercises His authority through us. If Christ—as the "Head"—wants satanic stones removed, He will do it through His "Hands": that is, through us, the believers. Note the expression: "a headship exercised throughout the Church, which is His body".

Christ has made us His "hands" on earth. He has empowered us and given us what it takes to remove satanic stones standing in our way. After His resurrection, He had some good news for His disciples: "All power is given unto me in heaven and in earth" (*Matthew 28:18, KJV*). Was He breaking this news to them merely to make them honour Him more? No! Rather, the news had something to do with *them.* "All power is given unto me" is as good as saying, "Believers, all power is given unto *you* in heaven and on earth." Oh, that's too big for you to digest! But let's go back to Ephesians chapter 1 again and see proofs of this:

> And [so that you can know and understand] what is the immeasurable and unlimited and surpassing greatness of His power in and for us who believe, as demonstrated in the working of His mighty strength...
>
> *Ephesians 1:19, AMPC*

The power is "in and for us who believe". Do you believe? If so, then the power is in you and for you—the power that dislodged the stone that wanted to control and retain Jesus in the grave. Are you a member of the Body of Christ? Are you the hands of Jesus? The power to remove the "stone" is in you right now. That is why Jesus is saying to you, "What are you waiting for? Take away the stone!"

It's for your use!

> Wherefore God also hath highly exalted him, and given him a name which is above every name: That at the name of Jesus every knee should bow, of things in heaven, and things in earth, and things under the earth; And that every tongue should confess that Jesus Christ is Lord, to the glory of God the Father.
>
> *Philippians 2:9-11, KJV*

Let's explore a little further why God expects you to be the one to "take away the stone". While God was giving Jesus power over all things, He had you and me in mind as well. In order for us to be partakers of this immeasurable power and authority, He made provision for "a name". What God did here was to give us the PIN or code for accessing this mighty power that resides in Christ.

It's all about us: "That at the name of Jesus every knee should bow." Who is going to mention the name? You don't expect Christ to say to the devil, "at my name, bow!" His presence alone is enough for the devil to bow. God made that provision of "at the name of Jesus" because of *us.* He put that section into the constitution of heaven so that we can "take away" every stone: those in heaven and on earth and under the earth.

Don't wait for the Lord to take away the stone. You are going to wait in vain. Sometimes I hear people pray, "God, come and remove this thing from our lives." No! Say instead, "I command you to be removed from my life, in the name of Jesus!" That's why we have the name, because it's for our use.

> But what does it say? "The word is near you, in your mouth and in your heart" (that is, the word of faith which we preach).
>
> *Romans 10:8, NKJV*

You have access to the mighty power of God; put it to good use, and begin to take away your stone. The name is in your mouth. There is a reason why God's Word says, "Thou shalt also decree a thing, and it shall be established unto thee: and the light shall shine upon thy ways" (*Job 22:28, KJV*). Our decrees are not empty declarations, but commands that carry the stamp of Christ through His name.

Get to work and begin to take away the satanic stone in the name of Jesus. Get to work and remove the stone, using the authority you have received by virtue of being a member of the Body of Christ. Open your mouth and begin to decree that the stone be removed, and "the light shall shine" upon you. Amen.

"This kind"

A boxing match typically consists of a determined number of three-minute rounds—a total of nine to twelve rounds. But, if you are a really good fighter or have a weak opponent, the fight can be won as early as the second round through a technical knockout; such bouts are said to have ended "inside the distance".

If you are knocked down during the fight—determined by whether you have touched the canvas floor of the ring with any part of your body other than your feet—the referee begins counting until you are back on your feet. Should you fail to get up by the count of ten, you will be ruled as knocked out, and your opponent will then be declared the winner by knockout. A technical knockout is possible as well, when the referee, fight doctor, or fighter's corner rules that a boxer is unable to safely continue to fight—whether due to injuries he has sustained or because he has been assessed as incapable of defending himself effectively.

Why am I bringing in this story about boxing? Because the same principle applies when it comes to removing satanic stones. Some forces, you can knock them out with "simple" prayers; but others will require fasting on top of prayer. To remove certain stones, you may have to do some fasting, or the Lord may need to prepare you through fasting so that you can give the enemy a technical knockout.

Jesus describes such opposition as "this kind". When the apostles came across this kind of stone and tried to remove it, they failed woefully:

And when they had come to the multitude, a man came to Him, kneeling down to Him and saying, "Lord, have mercy on my son, for he is an epileptic and suffers severely; for he often falls into the fire and often into the water. So I brought him to Your disciples, but they could not cure him."

Then Jesus answered and said, "O faithless and perverse generation, how long shall I be with you? How long shall I bear with you? Bring him here to Me."

And Jesus rebuked the demon, and it came out of him; and the child was cured from that very hour.

Then the disciples came to Jesus privately and said, "Why could we not cast it out?"

So Jesus said to them, "Because of your unbelief; for assuredly, I say to you, if you have faith as a mustard seed, you will say to this mountain, 'Move from here to there,' and it will move; and nothing will be impossible for you. **However, this kind does not go out except by prayer and fasting.**"

Matthew 17: 14-21, NKJV

You may be facing challenges caused by forces with elements of "this kind". They are stubborn and, to knock them out, you need to combine prayer with fasting. There have been times when the Spirit of the Lord would prompt me to fast, although I might not have any special need or issue to pray about. But those fasting periods have served as times of training to prepare me for the tough challenges ahead of me. Many times, I have looked back in victory and thanked God for toughening my spiritual muscles through prayer and fasting.

A friend of mine had problems getting married. She was advancing in age, but no man was coming to ask for her hand in marriage. She was beautiful, well-mannered and godly. But none of those qualities got her a husband. One day she decided to combine her prayer with fasting. For three days she waited on the Lord, in an attempt to "take away the stone". On the third day, she had a dream in which she saw her grandmother coming out of the grave and going into the family home. The old lady went into one of the rooms there, where there were pictures hanging on the walls.

She brought one of the picture frames down, and behind it was something tied up in a piece of cloth. The woman loosened the object, and the lady woke up with a happy feeling that she had been freed. Within a month, she met her husband. Today, she is happily married.

Not all opponents are the same: so, you will need the help of the Holy Spirit in dealing with the particular one troubling you. He will show you the most effective way to remove the stone. Receive the strength and wisdom of the Lord as you begin to remove this satanic stone from your life.

2. The Stone of Discontentment

"And blessed is he who is not offended because of Me."

Matthew 11:6, NKJV

Discontentment, or being offended with the Lord, can be a stone in the way of your getting your Lazarus. John had great expectations when He was thrown into prison: he expected Jesus to come to his rescue. But, when he didn't see Him, discontentment set in. Questions began to arise in his heart: "Maybe I was wrong when I described Him as the Lamb of God and the one whom Israel has been expecting." He sent his disciples to Jesus to enquire if Jesus was really "he that should come" (*Matthew 11:3, KJV*).

It was obvious that he was dissatisfied with the way Jesus had "handled his matter". He expected better treatment than what he got from the Lord. But Jesus said, "blessed is he who is not offended because of Me."

You are going to face situations where discontentment may become a stone in your life. You kept yourself chaste for your marriage bed, but you are still childless after many years of waiting. Your neighbour, who was busy sleeping around with men, had twins within nine months of her marriage. "Where is the reward of serving the Lord!" you may ask out of discontentment. You were the nice sister whom everyone described as the *virtuous woman*, but all the *bad girls* are now married and you don't even have a boyfriend. "Where is the reward of serving the Lord!" you ask.

You worked hard in school and served the Lord faithfully. The people who partied away their time and cheated in their exams all got good jobs after school, but you are still "just managing". You can't help but wonder, "Where is the reward of serving the Lord!" You spent years building the church but, when the time for ordination came, you were not considered. You just don't get it. "Where exactly is the reward of serving the Lord!" You never miss a prayer meeting or bible study, yet you aren't as prosperous as those "Sunday Christians" who are engrossed only in their work or business. It baffles you, and you can't help but ask, "Where is the reward of serving the Lord!"

Mary and Martha were at a point where the devil could have filled their hearts with discontentment: "Oh, when the Centurion asked Him to come and heal his servant, He was ready to go. But we sent for Him, and He failed to come—despite the fact that He uses our house for fellowship! What have we even benefited from our friendship with Him?"

When the Prodigal Son returned, the elder brother couldn't help but feel that his father had treated him unfairly. Out of discontentment, he grumbled to his father:

"Look! All these years I've been slaving for you and never disobeyed your orders. Yet you never gave me even a young goat so I could celebrate with my friends.

> But when this son of yours who has squandered your property with prostitutes comes home, you kill the fattened calf for him!"
>
> *Luke 15: 29-30*

In Malachi chapter 3 we see a similar scenario, with the people concluding that "it is futile to serve God":

> "You have said, 'It is futile to serve God. What do we gain by carrying out his requirements...? But now we call the arrogant blessed. Certainly evildoers prosper, and even when they put God to the test, they get away with it.'"
>
> *Malachi 3:14-15*

Do you harbour such thoughts too? Paint mental pictures of unfaithful people you know, who have received the blessings of a faithful Father? Feel bitter with the way God is handling your case? Do something about this stone of discontentment! Recall His words, ""blessed is he who is not offended because of Me." I have gone through experiences where I have had to deal with this stone of discontentment, of being offended with the Lord. It's a terrible stone to deal with but, with God's grace, you will be able to remove it.

3. The Stone of Guilt for Past Misdeeds

This is another stone that stands in the Lord's way. Many times, the devil continues to accuse us (*Revelation 12:10*) of past sins that we have already confessed to God and for which we have already received His forgiveness. This causes us to live with the notion that our predicament and the delays to our prayers are the result of divine punishment for our past sins.

While David was running away from Absalom, Shimei came after him. He cast stones at David and his servants. He also hurled insults at David, saying:

> "The LORD has repaid you for all the blood you shed in the household of Saul, in whose place you have reigned. The LORD has given the kingdom into the hands of your son Absalom. You have come to ruin because you are a murderer!"
>
> *2 Samuel 16:8*

Strangely enough, King David allowed this impudence to go unpunished, and he stopped Abishai from cutting off the head of "this dead dog" (*2 Samuel 16:9*). What made the king swallow such ridicule? He was living with the belief that it was God who had permitted him to be insulted because of his past sin!

> "So let him curse, because the LORD has said to him, 'Curse David.' Who then shall say, 'Why have you done so?'"
>
> *2 Samuel 16:10, NKJV*

> "Let him alone, and let him curse; for so the LORD has ordered him."
>
> *2 Samuel 16:11, NKJV*

There are believers who believe the Lord has not blessed them with a spouse because they had an abortion before they came to Him. Others live with the notion that God is causing them to have a hard time because they didn't serve Him enough when they were younger. Still others are of the view that their problem is God's way of reminding them of past misdeeds committed against Him. Like David, they are saying, "Let it alone... this problem is divine punishment."

They are waiting for the day when "God will at last be willing to forgive me... maybe, on that day, my problems will come to an end".

Sometimes the devil reminds us of our past sins, but we think it is the Holy Spirit speaking to us. So, you get down on your knees and pray, "Lord, once again I ask for mercy concerning this evil deed..." How many times are you going to confess, before you realize you *have* already been forgiven? God's forgiveness is not based on the number of times we ask.

It is important that we take away this stone of a negative image of God, and see Him for who He really is: a loving and compassionate Father who forgives the sins and transgressions of all who come to Him. This is what He says to us:

> "I, even I, am he who blots out your transgressions, for my own sake, and remembers your sins no more."
>
> *Isaiah 43:25*

Do not allow the spirit of Shimei—the erroneous thought that your predicament is a result of divine judgment—any foothold in your life. David spared this man, but his son Solomon didn't spare him. Shimei's malicious curses left a big sore in the heart of David, so much so that he couldn't help but remind Solomon of him while he was on his deathbed (*1 Kings 2:8-9*). Do something about those guilty thoughts, and do not let the enemy capitalize on them to rob you of your blessings:

> Casting down imaginations... and bringing into captivity every thought to the obedience of Christ...
>
> *2 Corinthians 10:5*

4. The Stone of "My Destiny"

Thank God for His revelatory messages about our destiny. Unfortunately, the devil has gotten many into trouble by deceiving them into believing *his* false messages about their "destiny", instead of what God is saying to them.

I remember a friend who got into serious difficulties because the devil had twisted her life so badly that she wished she were dead. In the course of talking to her, I noticed that this dear child of God kept repeating a particular phrase: "It's destiny." In other words, she believed that she was "destined" to go through those harrowing experiences and there was apparently nothing anyone could have done to avert the evil that had befallen her.

Was it really her destiny? No! It was the devil at work in her life. This lady was bitter with God for "giving" her such a "destiny". But it was not a matter of "destiny" at all; it was the devil's handiwork.

God does not plan bad destinies for His children. Jesus told Peter, "Satan hath desired to have you" (*Luke 22:31, KJV*). The devil wanted Peter to be tagged as "that brother that used to follow Jesus but has now gone back to the world." He knew that God's real destiny for Peter was to make him a pillar in His kingdom, but he was bent on destroying this plan.

"It's my destiny" is an evil imagination that we must remove from our way, if we want Lazarus to come forth. The devil wants us to continue living with this idea and be resigned to our plight. He will try to stop you from pressing forward towards your deliverance and freedom. God, on the other hand, wants you to take this stone away, so that He can restore Lazarus to you.

If your so-called "destiny" does not give you peace and hope, then it's not of the Lord:

> "For I know the thoughts and plans that I have for you, says the Lord, thoughts and plans for welfare and peace and not for evil, to give you hope in your final outcome."
>
> *Jeremiah 29:11, AMPC*

That's your destiny! Change your imagination today: remove every negative thought about your destiny and look ahead with hope to God's plans for your welfare and peace.

5. The Stone of Self-Disqualification

"I don't qualify" is another stone that the devil plants in our hearts to prevent us from receiving our Lazarus. There are Christians who think they haven't done enough to "qualify" for certain blessings. They look at other people and say, "If only I can serve in the church like this brother, then God will love me more and take care of my problem. If only I can fast like that sister, then God will meet all my needs."

Even though God wants to do something for these people, they are not ready to receive His help—because they are too busy trying to do "enough" to "make" God consider them "fit" for His blessings. But the truth is, if you have accepted Christ as your Saviour, you are already "fit"; you don't have to do anything else. The first and paramount qualification for God's blessings is acceptance into the family of God through the blood of Christ:

> Giving thanks to the Father, who has qualified and made us fit to share the portion which is the inheritance of the saints (God's holy people) in the Light.
>
> *Colossians 1:12, AMPC*

Christ has made us "fit". He has "qualified" as many as received Him as Lord and Saviour:

> But as many as received Him, to them He gave the right to become children of God, to those who believe in His name...
>
> *John 1:12, NKJV*

It is important for us to live with the mindset that we became Christians *by grace* and will remain Christians *by grace*. As the apostle Paul once put it:

> But by the grace of God I am what I am, and his grace to me was not without effect. No, I worked harder than all of them—yet not I, but the grace of God that was with me.
>
> *1 Corinthians 15:10*

Paul was aware that all he had achieved was "by the grace of God". It is the grace and mercy of God that qualifies you. Some, who think it is their own self-effort that "qualifies" them in the sight of God, oftentimes don't even receive His best. They are like the Pharisee who went into the presence of God with his spiritual resume and boasted of his good deeds—only to leave without any blessing (*Luke 18:9-14*).

The people Christ chose to be His disciples were not those who, in the eyes of men, qualified for such a high calling. They were unlearned folks. Jesus said:

> I thank You, Father... that You have hidden these things from the wise and clever and learned, and revealed them to babies [to the childish, untaught, and unskilled].
>
> *Matthew 11:25, AMPC*

Peter didn't qualify to raise the dead. It was Jesus who qualified him. David didn't qualify to take the place of Saul. God qualified him. Moses didn't qualify to stand before a world leader like Pharaoh, but God qualified him.

Paul said, "I don't give room for laziness. I work harder than anyone else. But even the ability to work hard is a function of grace." Grace made him a tireless worker for God. Grace made him a successful worker; that was why he was quick to say, "by the grace of God I am what I am."

If even such a great apostle as Paul realized that all he needed was God's grace, why then do you allow the devil to whisper to you that you don't qualify for God's blessings? There can be no greater qualification for your blessings than Christ's death on the cross, which made you a joint heir with Him. See Christ as your greatest qualification. When God sees Christ in you, He sees a child of His, one that qualifies for all His blessings.

> Blessed be the God and Father of our Lord Jesus Christ, who hath blessed us with all spiritual blessings in heavenly places in Christ...
>
> *Ephesians 1:3, KJV*

We qualify for "all spiritual blessings" that God has made available to us—not by our own efforts, but "in Christ". That's what the Bible says. When the Prodigal Son returned to his father and tried to tell him that he wasn't worthy to be called his son or to receive the blessings of a son, his father didn't pay any attention to his words. The only thing on his mind was to shower his son with love and restore him to his original position—the position of sonship and not of servanthood (*Luke 15:21-24*). It's time you rid yourself of every imagination that makes you feel unworthy of God's blessings. That's a stone of the devil. The Lord is saying, "Take away the stone," and then He will command Lazarus to come forth.

6. The Stone of Motives

> Then the LORD saw that the wickedness of man was great in the earth, and that every intent of the thoughts of his heart was only evil continually.
>
> *Genesis 6:5, NKJV*

Another stone that the Lord expects His children to take away is that of evil motives. God is not only mindful of what we say and do, He is also very mindful of our intentions and thoughts. Sometimes our words may be pleasing, but our thoughts and motives may be bad. People can be taken in by our outward show, but God examines both our actions and motives.

What disqualified Eliab from becoming king of Israel? He seemed to be the ideal candidate: he had the stature of a king and a leader. But when God looked at the contents of his heart, He shook His head and told Samuel, "Everything looks alright on the outside, but I am not comfortable with what I am seeing behind this impressive facade."

> For the Lord sees not as man sees; for man looks on the outward appearance, but the Lord looks on the heart.
>
> *1 Samuel 16:7, AMPC*

God looks at the heart to see the motives therein. People may say, "Oh, he really loves the Lord." But God knows that this man only loves his pocket and all his zealous labour is merely a ploy to get himself promoted.

When Judas protested about the costly perfume that Mary poured on Jesus' feet, he sounded like someone genuinely interested in the welfare of the poor. But his protest was born out of greed: he was a thief who wanted the perfume to be sold so that he could steal the money, as he had been habitually doing:

> Then Mary took about a pint of pure nard, an expensive perfume; she poured it on Jesus' feet and wiped his feet with her hair. And the house was filled with the fragrance of the perfume.
>
> But one of his disciples, Judas Iscariot, who was later to betray him, objected, "Why wasn't this perfume sold and the money given to the poor? It was worth a year's wages."
>
> He did not say this because he cared about the poor but because he was a thief; as keeper of the money bag, he used to help himself to what was put into it.
>
> *John 12:3-6*

When God takes a look at your motives, does He see love? Or nothing but schemes and treacherous tendencies? "Oh, she's very helpful to the pastor and the brethren." But God looks at her heart, and He sees a stronghold of manipulation and devilish plots.

> Ye ask, and receive not, because ye ask amiss, that ye may consume it upon your lusts.
>
> *James 4:3, KJV*

If you want God to bring Lazarus out, you will need to do something about the stone of evil motives in your heart.

7. The Stone of Sin

Therefore… let us lay aside every weight, and the sin which so easily ensnares us, and let us run with endurance the race that is set before us…

Hebrews 12:1, NKJV

The last stone I want us to look at is the stone of sin. *Hebrews 12:1* tells us to "lay aside" the sin which ensnares us. That's the same as telling us to take it away. Do you want Lazarus restored? You will have to take away your sin first, before God can step in to help you. Sin, according to this verse, "ensnares" us. The New International Version puts it as "hinders". Sin is a stone that hinders God from getting your Lazarus out.

There are people who want God to help them, but they are not ready to lay aside their sins. You want God to give you a God-fearing man, but you can't lay aside fornication and anger. You will make life miserable for His son. Lay aside that stone, and He will intervene in your situation.

You have been praying for "a good wife" but you are living a life of lies and deceit, which doesn't make you look like a suitable husband for "a good wife". You will give His daughter nights of pain if He were to give her to you.

You want God to make you wealthy, but He sees the way you are robbing Him through failure to pay your tithes. Lay aside that stone of sin, and you will see His glory.

The night is far spent, the day is at hand: let us therefore cast off the works of darkness, and let us put on the armour of light.

Romans 13:12, KJV

"Cast off" is another way of saying, "take away the stone". If you want God to deliver you from the power of darkness, you must lay aside the unfruitful works of darkness (*Ephesians 5:11*). Sin puts us and our blessings under the control of the power of darkness.

> Giving thanks unto the Father... Who hath delivered us from the power of darkness, and hath translated us into the kingdom of his dear Son...
>
> *Colossians 1:13*

If you want God to bring Lazarus out, then you will have to be on His side. His hands are not shortened, that He can't save you. His ear is not heavy, that it can't hear you. So, what's the problem? It's this:

> But your iniquities have separated you from your God; your sins have hidden his face from you, so that he will not hear.
>
> *Isaiah 59:2*

That's the problem. Take away the stone of sin, and He will turn His attention to you. The process of building and restoration begins with taking away the stone of sin: "If thou return to the Almighty, thou shalt be built up, thou shalt put away iniquity far from thy tabernacles" (*Job 22:23, KJV*). Notice what you have to do to iniquity, to be built up: put it far away from you.

> If my people, which are called by my name, shall humble themselves, and pray, and seek my face, and turn from their wicked ways; then will I hear from heaven, and will forgive their sin, and will heal their land.
>
> *2 Chronicles 7:14, KJV*

First and foremost, we must turn from our wicked (sinful) ways. It is only then that God will hear from heaven and heal every area of our lives where we are having a problem—whether it's our marriage, home or job.

Don't allow the devil to continue to cheat and lie to you. Don't fall for the lies of preachers who tell you, "Just sow that seed, and God is going to solve your problem." God is more interested in having you remove the stone of sin than your giving Him a fat seed. Jesus didn't die for your seed, He died to have you redeemed from the clutches of sin. God told Cain:

> "If you do what is right, will you not be accepted? But if you do not do what is right, sin is crouching at your door; it desires to have you, but you must rule over it."
>
> *Genesis 4:7*

If you do what is right, by taking away the stone of sin, you will be accepted. God will step in, and you will have your Lazarus restored.

Many of our problems have nothing to do with demons; it's just a matter of sin. Sometimes people say, "That witch in my neighbourhood is responsible for my predicament." No, it is that sin in your body that is responsible. Some are busy binding evil spirits, when all that God requires them to do is the simple act of *taking away the stone of bitterness, pride, malice, envy or disobedience.*

You may not need a forty-day fast. You may not need some special revival programme. Just take away that stone of sin that the Holy Spirit has been talking to you about, and the Lord will make Lazarus come forth for you.

8

The Magnitude of the Problem

Martha, the sister of him that was dead, said to him, Lord, by this time he stinks: for he has been dead four days.

John 11:39b, AKJV

Just when the Lord was about to step into the situation, just when Lazarus was about to come out of the grave, the devil began to paint pictures of impossibility in the heart of Martha. A fresh battle began to build up in her mind. When she couldn't hold it in anymore, she voiced her objections: "Lord, by this time he stinks."

The devil had given her an x-ray of the situation, and she was presenting the result to the Lord. She was telling Him, "Let's forget about this; the situation is now beyond remedy. We are aware of Jairus' daughter and the son of the woman of Nain, but this is a peculiar case. By now he stinks."

Many today are saying the same thing to the Lord: "We have the doctor's report; they say this case is different"; "I have no womb, this is not the same situation as Hannah's or Sarah's"; "My husband is a chronic womanizer and a drunkard, this is not a marriage that can be fixed."

"By this time, he stinks" means: by this time, it has passed the point where one might nurse any hope of something good coming out of the situation. It means all is lost.

There's no point putting up a fight anymore—just accept your fate and endure the situation. There are people out there who are no longer seeking or believing God for the solution to their problems. They are merely "enduring" it and asking for the "grace" to endure to the end. They have given up all hope. The devil has told them, "By now, it stinks." There was a time when they were all fired up with hope, praying and trusting God for His intervention. But nothing happened, and they have come to the conclusion that "by this time, it stinks".

Full of hope and vigour, Moses dreamt of delivering the Israelites from slavery in Egypt. But he made the mistake of killing an Egyptian who had beaten one of his fellowmen. The outcome was disastrous, as he had to flee Egypt when his secret act came to light. Years later, he was a lonely shepherd with an office on the backside of a desert. His lofty dream of being Israel's deliverer had long been buried and was already stinking when he encountered God.

God came and told him, "I'm sending you to Pharaoh." But Moses no longer had any zeal or faith to believe Him. All he had left was a bag full of excuses: "By now it stinks," was what he was saying to the Lord.

What has time and the flood of past defeats done to you? God still has a plan for that project you think has been abandoned. He still has a plan for that home you think has totally crumbled. He still has plans for that project you think you will never get back to.

In the mind of Martha, Lazarus was a "stinking" project: a project that didn't require faith or further attention. But Jesus didn't see a stinking Lazarus. He saw a healthy young man who would become a source of wonder to his world.

It takes only a few seconds for the devil to dupe us into seeing a different picture and making a negative confession. Within seconds, the devil had removed the picture of God's power and love from Martha's mind and replaced it with something else: now she was seeing Lazarus as the Promised Land that can never be reached.

Oh, she will tell you that she can now "see the true picture of things". She will say to you that she has done "a rational analysis of the situation" and can now tell that she is up against "a really impossible task": *by now it stinks!*

Aren't you saying and doing the same thing? "When I was in my twenties, I looked really ravishing and there was hope of attracting a man and getting married. But now, I'm not sure." "Back in the days, it was easy to get a job once you graduated. But now, you must have connections, and I don't have any." *By now it stinks!*

There are nights when the devil will wake you up for a hard talk about your "stinking" situation. He will show you the "true picture of things" so that you won't "disturb and deceive" yourself. He will give you many "valid" reasons why you should quit following Christ to that grave of Lazarus with the hope of receiving a miracle from Him. These are the times when you will need your shield of faith to quench the enemy's fiery darts.

Might This Thing Be...?

Jesus had said earlier, "I am the resurrection, and the life" (*John 11:25*). And Martha had replied, "Yes, Lord, I believe..." But right at the tomb of Lazarus, the devil had whispered in her ear, "Even if He said He is the resurrection and the life, what can He do about this corpse, when *by now it stinks*?"

Is it possible to bring Lazarus out, without the stench chasing people away? Wouldn't this be a very hard ground to tread? That was the idea the devil was trying to sell to her.

The Bible tells us about a time when there was a great famine in Samaria. It was so severe that people started eating up their own children (*2 Kings 6:28-29*). But in the middle of this stinking situation, God spoke through Elisha: "Tomorrow about this time a measure of fine flour will sell for a shekel and two measures of barley for a shekel in the gate of Samaria" (*2 Kings 7:1, AMPC*). What he was saying was that, within 24 hours, good food would again be readily available, and for a small fraction of the price the people had been paying during the famine.

It sounded too good to be true; so impossible that the king's officer retorted, "Look, even if the LORD should open the floodgates of the heavens, could this happen?" To this, Elisha replied, "You will see it with your own eyes... but you will not eat any of it" (*2 Kings 7:2*). The officer's negative remark had ruled him out of partaking in that great miracle!

At the tomb of Lazarus, we see the same spirit at work, trying to talk Martha out of believing the Lord: "He can be a miracle worker, but *might this thing be?*"

"Yes, He divided the Red Sea and brought water out of the rock, but is He going to deliver us from the giants? *Might this thing be?*" Whenever God wants to do something great in your life, the devil will try to find a way of putting this question in your mind: *"Might this thing be?"*

Dealing with Doubts and Fears

Then Jesus said, "Did I not tell you that if you believe, you will see the glory of God?"

John 11:40

Jesus could see that fear and doubt had set in. To bring Lazarus out of the grave, He had to uproot fear and doubt from the hearts of Martha and her sister.

> But when you ask, you must believe and not doubt, because the one who doubts is like a wave of the sea, blown and tossed by the wind. That person should not expect to receive anything from the Lord.
>
> *James 1:6-7*

Christ had to get them to the point of believing and thereby pleasing God, for "without faith it is impossible to please God" (*Hebrews 11:6*). How did He do it?

Remember!

Remember. This was the key that Christ used to root out the spirit of fear and doubt. Many times, we try to bind the spirit of fear and doubt; but here, Christ shows us a simple, yet effective method of dealing with fear and doubt—*remember!*

When fears and doubts take hold of your heart, try to "remember". Jesus didn't bind or cast out any spirit, He merely turned the attention of the doubtful and fearful Martha to the things He had told her earlier: "Did I not tell you?" For fear and doubt to give way to faith and courage, Martha had to recall and meditate on the things the Lord had told her in times past. This was exactly what God was getting her to do: "Remember what I told you." Paul said it well:

> Finally, brothers and sisters, whatever is true, whatever is noble, whatever is right, whatever is pure, whatever is lovely, whatever is admirable—if anything is excellent or praiseworthy—think about such things.
>
> *Philippians 4:8*

The devil is good at getting into our thoughts and presenting us with the "factual" state of our problems; convincing us that our problems have reached a "stinking" stage beyond any remedy. But it is at such a point that we need to "remember". What exactly has God said to you in the past? What exactly has He said to you in His Word, at a church service, when you were praying, or during a time of fellowship? As Paul said, "Think about such things."

There have been occasions when I spent quality time recalling things that the Lord had told me earlier. This helps me get rid of fear, doubt and discouragement in the face of unfavourable circumstances. Sometimes, God shows or tells us things in advance so that they can serve as an anchor for our faith later on when are going through challenges.

Genesis chapter 32 gives an example of this: Jacob comes face to face with the man he fears most—his brother Esau—and knows that danger was imminent. He is "greatly afraid and distressed" (*Genesis 32:7, KJV*). But, amid his fear and distress, he casts his mind back to an encounter he once had with God—and to words that God had spoken to him then, words that now give him hope in the midst of his present predicament. So, he prays:

> O God of my father Abraham and God of my father Isaac, the Lord Who said to me, Return to your country and to your people and I will do you good...
>
> *Genesis 32:9, AMPC*

This was an effective prayer born out of the simple act of remembrance. Jesus wanted Martha to come to this point of remembering what He had said to her about believing in Him and seeing the glory of God.

Keep in mind the things the Lord says to you. One of the works the Holy Spirit does in our life is to remind us of what the Lord has said to us:

> But the Helper, the Holy Spirit, whom the Father will send in My name, He will teach you all things, and bring to your remembrance all things that I said to you.
>
> *John 14:26, NKJV*

Don't ignore the remembrance sessions that the Holy Spirit takes you through. Don't always seek new revelations and messages from the Lord. Sometimes, you need only to recall the old message to come out of your present predicament. The Israelites got into trouble and couldn't receive all the good things God had planned for them because they failed to "remember": "Our fathers... did not remember the multitude of Your mercies, but rebelled by the sea—the Red Sea" (*Psalm 106:7, NKJV*).

> How oft did they provoke him in the wilderness, and grieve him in the desert! Yea, they turned back and tempted God, and limited the Holy One of Israel. They remembered not his hand, nor the day when he delivered them from the enemy.
>
> *Psalm 78:40-42, KJV*

Had Martha remembered what the Lord said to her earlier, Lazarus could have got out of the grave sooner. The time Jesus had to spend, giving her a fresh sermon on faith, wouldn't have been necessary. You will speed up your miracle if you spend time recalling what the Lord said to you earlier. This is one sure way of dealing with doubt and fear, an effective way of keeping the fire of your faith aglow.

9

Moving the Lord through Obedience

Then they took away the stone from the place where the dead man was lying. And Jesus lifted up His eyes and said, "Father, I thank You that You have heard Me."

John 11:41, NKJV

The Lord has been at the residence of this bereaved family for some time. He has wept over the situation and even given a faith-lifting sermon on resurrection. He has also been at the grave for some time. But nothing has really changed. No miracle. Nothing to rejoice over.

Why would the Lord hang around us and not do anything to change our situation? Sometimes, as we see in this case, it is because our obedience is incomplete. In fact, it has been God's will all along to deal with the forces holding Lazarus back, but He requires Mary and Martha to come to the point where their "obedience is complete" (*2 Corinthians 10:6*). Until then, there is little He can do.

To have our miracle, we need not only faith but also obedience. God may be saying to you, "Quit that relationship, and I will open a new door for you." But, as long as you find it hard to say, "OK, I will," there is little He can do, even with your ceaseless nights of prayer and confession.

Obedience is the key to having your Lazarus back. Christ may weep with you over your Lazarus but, if your obedience is not complete, there is little He can do about restoring Lazarus to you. *Isaiah 1:19* tells us, "If you are willing and obedient, you will eat the good things of the land." Eating the good things of the land is tied to your obedience. I see the Lord standing at the tomb of Lazarus, just waiting for His children to obey His instructions so that He can go ahead to give them the miracle they desire.

Are you willing to obey? The Bible says that, the moment they came to that point of obedience, Jesus lifted His eyes and began to discuss the situation with His Father. You see, Jesus had His eyes on the problem and their feelings all this while, but it was their obedience that prompted Him to look up to the hill from whence comes help (*Psalm 121:1*).

I want you to notice what Christ said: "Father, I thank You that You have heard Me." Jesus had already discussed the matter with God, even before coming to Bethany, and had been given the assurance that Lazarus would come back to life. There was only one thing left that would move Him to swing into action: the sisters' obedience. Your blessing is ready. Your prayers have already been answered. But check yourself: *is your obedience complete?*

Disobedience is a tool that Satan often uses to cheat God's children of their blessings. Man's first test was a test of obedience, and he failed it woefully (see *Genesis 2:16-17; 3:1-6*). For generations, the children of Israel found it hard to fully enjoy God's manifold provisions for them because they couldn't pass the test of obedience. God had good plans for them, but those plans were tied to their obedience.

God would say, "Turn right, and I will bless you," and they would say, "No, we'd rather go left." Note what God said:

> "Now if you obey me fully and keep my covenant, then out of all nations you will be my treasured possession. Although the whole earth is mine, you will be for me a kingdom of priests and a holy nation."
>
> *Exodus 19:5-6*

Great promises, but they came attached with a condition: "If you obey me fully." Do you want God's blessings? Obedience is the key.

> And you shall return and obey the voice of the Lord and do all His commandments which I command you today.
>
> And the Lord your God will make you abundantly prosperous in every work of your hand, in the fruit of your body, of your cattle, of your land, for good; for the Lord will again delight in prospering you, as He took delight in your fathers...
>
> *Deuteronomy 30:8-9, AMPC*

God describes Jesus as the One in whom He is well pleased (*Matthew 3:17*). You know why? Because of His obedience to the Father:

> And being found in appearance as a man, He humbled Himself and became obedient to the point of death, even the death of the cross.
>
> *Philippians 2:8, NKJV*

In *Isaiah 42:1*, God describes Jesus as "my servant". What is the duty of a servant? Obedience to his master. Obedience to God makes Him your ally. Samuel told the Israelites that it was more profitable to obey the Lord than to disobey Him.

"If you fear the LORD and serve and obey him and do not rebel against his commands, and if both you and the king who reigns over you follow the LORD your God—good!

"But if you do not obey the LORD, and if you rebel against his commands, his hand will be against you, as it was against your ancestors."

1 Samuel 12:14-15

It's a great thing to have the Lord on your side. It may not always be easy to obey Him, but it pays to do so. The blessings are numerous, and it's the surest way to the top!

"At Your Word"

Simon answered and said to Him, "Master, we have toiled all night and caught nothing; nevertheless at Your word I will let down the net."

Luke 5:5, NKJV

Like Mary and Martha, Simon had reached a stage of thorough despondency; he had come to that point where the battle seemed lost. His skills had failed him. He was a hard worker, but sometimes diligence can fail you. The battle is not to the strong. You can be a skilful and diligent fisherman, but the devil can drive the fish to the other side of the sea, where your net won't find them.

It had been a tortuous night for Simon, and he was ready to return home empty-handed. Only one thing still kept him waiting: The Master was making use of his boat. Once the sermon was over, Simon was ready to go home. But the Lord told him, "Wait a minute, take me to the grave. I want to bring your Lazarus out of the grave."

Simon's reaction was no different from Martha's. He began to give the Lord facts and figures: "I have toiled all night and caught nothing. I have reached a point where there is no need to try anymore. Just say 'thank you' for the boat and let me go."

But Simon (whom Christ later renamed Peter) didn't simply stop at that point of despair. He took a step further: he took his eyes away from the empty net and ignored the spirit whispering to him about the "stinking" situation, and he got down to the point of obedience: "Things look hopeless but, at Your word, I will let down my net."

That was what Christ had been waiting to hear. He had a big reward for Simon Peter, for letting Him use his boat, but it was a reward that could only be received by obedience. Had Peter left without obeying the Lord, he would never have experienced that net-breaking miracle.

"At Your word" opens the door to having your Lazarus back. Mary had a very important piece of advice for the people who ran out of wine at the marriage in Cana: "Do whatever he tells you" (*John 2:5*). So, they took Him at His word, and they got six pots of wine.

For Naaman, it was ""Go, wash yourself seven times in the Jordan, and your flesh will be restored and you will be cleansed" (*2 Kings 5:10*). Naaman didn't like the idea; he had expected Elisha to come out and call on the name of the Lord and wave his hand over the leprous spot. He would have died of leprosy had he left in a rage—as he did at first—but his recovery came when he turned back and chose to say, "At Your word, I will…" So, he got a brand-new skin as a reward for his obedience.

"Then they took away the stone from the place where the dead man was lying. And Jesus lifted up His eyes and said..." Jesus lifted His eyes and prayed only after their act of obedience. You too can make Jesus lift up His eyes through your obedience.

Take a little time and reflect on your walk with the Lord. Could there be areas where your lack of obedience is hindering you from receiving your Lazarus? You want financial blessings, but you don't want to obey His instructions on tithing and giving. There is little that you can get from Him in terms of financial blessings. You want Him to deal with your enemies, but you are unwilling to obey His word on forgiveness. There is little that He can do for you.

Or could there be conflicts between you and your spouse that are hindering your prayers? Perhaps you, as a husband, need to treat your wife with more consideration and honour (*1 Peter 3:7*). Or perhaps God might just be requiring you, as a wife, to obey Him by submitting to your husband (*Ephesians 5:22-33*). Simple obedience here could just be the key to unlocking your long-awaited miracle. Do not harden your heart (*Hebrews 3:8*) when He speaks to you.

Years ago, God sent my father on an evangelistic mission to a new place of ministry. We had to move with him, which meant changing schools. When I enrolled at my new school, I was asked to repeat the class I had graduated from at my previous school. I thought about my former classmates and felt sad because they would be a class ahead of me. I didn't like the idea, so I told my parents that I wanted to go back to my former school to avoid repeating the class at my new school.

They pleaded with me to persevere in the new environment I had been placed in, but at first my pride wouldn't allow me to accede to their request. However, I did give in eventually: I decided to stay in that new school and repeat the class.

That was the turning point in my studies. For the first time in my life, I rose above the level of mediocrity. Up till then, I had been just an average student in class, but it seemed like God made me smarter from that time onwards, and I began to comprehend things better than before. For the first time ever, I topped my class—even though the academic standard at this new school was higher than at my former school. God also opened doors for me to represent my new school at interschool competitions, where I won awards. I also appeared on television several times.

It was a great experience for me at that age, and those years shaped my life and my future. At the time I had to repeat the class, I didn't know it was all part of God's plan for me. The only thought in my young mind then was that my classmates in my former school would be "ahead" of me. They were never really ahead of me, anyway. God had better plans for me, but I would have missed out on them if I had not obeyed my parents, who were His voice to me.

There always comes a point when your miracle will not depend on what God is willing to do, but what you are ready to do. Go ahead and obey Him. Then He will restore your Lazarus to you.

10

Christ's Victorious Approach

Jesus lifted up His eyes and said, "Father, I thank You that You have heard Me. And I know that You always hear Me…

John 11:41-42, NKJV

Jesus had a very successful ministry, one that can serve as a pattern for us. A key reason for His success can be found in these words: "Father… You always hear Me." Imagine what your life and ministry would be like if the Father always hears you. For Christ, there was never any fear of defeat; victory was always certain.

You might be thinking: "Of course, victory would always be certain for *Him*; after all, He *is* God's beloved Son!" But, in fact, His success was due more to the way He approached God than to anything else. *John 11:41-42* gives us an insight into Christ's successful approach, and I will now touch on this, because I believe we can be just as successful when we apply the same approach. This short passage of Scripture— only two verses long—contains a model prayer: an effective prayer which resulted in one of the greatest miracles ever.

A Father-Son Consciousness

What was the first word that Christ uttered in prayer at the tomb of Lazarus?

It was *"Father!"* Fifteen times, Christ used this name in prayer. Why? Because He had a "Father-Son consciousness". He regarded God as His Father; He went before Him as His Son. He made His request with the faith a child has when making a request of his father. He never approached God with the consciousness of a man in desperate need of help from a superior power. He approached God with the consciousness of a *Son.*

The Jews had a problem with this. They considered it a sacrilege for Jesus to regard God as His Father. They had a warped concept of God, viewing Him through the lenses of their own religiosity. No wonder Jesus told them that they didn't know the Father. If they had known God as their Father, they would have related differently with Him.

The world, too, does not know who God really is. As Jesus said, in a later prayer: "O righteous Father, the world doesn't know you, but I do; and these disciples know you sent me" (*John 17:25, TLB*). But is not only the Jews or the world who have not known the Father; many people in the Church have not known the Father either. This explains the way they approach Him in prayer.

My father was one of the kindest men I have ever met. But, while we were growing up, he handled us with a very firm hand. I am thankful for that, because we lived in an environment where He needed to be firm with us. However, our love for him was mixed with dread. Those of us who were his older, "first-generation" children knew him as a stern father. He had a cane for us and never "spared the rod"! But, by the time his two youngest, "new-generation" children came into the world, my father had discarded his dreaded cane.

Those two youngest siblings of mine related with my father differently. While the rest of us used to approach him in fear to make our modest requests, those two would walk up to him confidently and make extravagant demands—which he gladly met. They even cracked jokes with him, and he would laugh heartily. We, the "first generation" children, never dared to do that! We still carried our image of him as a "stern" father in our minds, and this robbed us of many good things we would otherwise have received from him. Sometimes we bottled up our needs and, whenever he discovered this, it would grieve him. "Why didn't you tell me?" he would ask. But we were afraid.

Throughout my schooldays, I never complained to my father that the pocket money he gave me wasn't enough. But those two "new-generation" children had no qualms about telling him, "this money won't be enough," and he would gladly give them as much as they asked for. I also saw how my father would often stop over at their school, when his itinerary permitted it, and give them whatever they wanted. They had more from him, because they had in their mind a picture of a loving father, and they had confidence in his presence—unlike those of us who carried an image of him as a hard man!

When Jesus came, He wanted us to know God and approach Him as our Father—both in our relationship with Him and in prayer. The hard-line approach of God in the wilderness is not all that there is about the nature of God. The mighty thunder and lightning of Sinai, which caused the Israelites to dread approaching God, is not all that there is about the Father. But that was the picture many of the Jews had of God.

So, when Paul wrote about approaching God, he made it clear that the Sinai experience should not form the basis of our present relationship with God. Read what he said:

> For you have not come [as did the Israelites in the wilderness] to a mountain that can be touched, [a mountain] that is ablaze with fire, and to gloom and darkness and a raging storm, and to the blast of a trumpet and a voice whose words make the listeners beg that nothing more be said to them.
>
> For they could not bear the command that was given: If even a wild animal touches the mountain, it shall be stoned to death. In fact, so awful and terrifying was the [phenomenal] sight that Moses said, I am terrified (aghast and trembling with fear).
>
> *Hebrews 12:18-21, AMPC*

Those Israelites saw only the stern, terrifying side of God and missed the greater and most vital part of Him: His loving, fatherly nature. But Jesus wanted His disciples to think of God differently, as their loving Father. He wanted them to have the same result that He was having when He prayed—just like my "new-generation" siblings, who approached my father with confidence and got more from him! So, when the disciples asked Him to teach them how to pray, the first thing He taught them was to address God as "Our Father".

Yes, He is our Maker. Yes, He is our King. Yes, He is our Judge. But, when we enter His presence, we must enter with the consciousness that He is "Our Father". He wants to be worshipped as a Father; He wants to be loved as a Father; and He wants us to ask things of Him as Our Father—not as a group of fearful, beggarly and desperate people.

The writer of Hebrews also exhorted Christians to have a Father-son consciousness in their approach to God. Approaching God, he said, is coming to "Mount Zion, even to the city of the living God, the heavenly Jerusalem, and to countless multitudes of angels in festal gathering…" (*Hebrews 12:22, AMPC*).

When I go to my son's class to bring him back from school, I am excited by the way he jumps up from his seat, leaving every other business behind him, and runs into my outstretched arms. Other children don't do that to me; they only stand and stare, wishing it was their father who had come. When we walk out of the gate, he holds my hand and pulls me in the direction of the kiosk and picks out whatever he wants from it. He doesn't ask me if I have the money to pay. He just picks whatever he wants and lets me take care of the bill! What gives him the courage to do all of that? It is the "father-son" consciousness in him! No other child in his school can do that with me. That's what Jesus wants us to have when we enter God's presence in prayer.

Without this consciousness, it is difficult to approach God and get results. It is difficult to even have faith in God. Why? Because you are not sure whether He is going to be favourably disposed to you. You might be afraid of approaching your boss to ask for a pay rise. You might be afraid of approaching your landlord to ask for extra time to pay your rent. But, if you have a loving and generous father, you can go before him confidently and make your request. No fear. No doubt. Because you know who your father is.

Many times, when Christ was teaching His disciples how to pray, He tried to drive home this point: *have a Father-son consciousness in your relationship with God.*

Note how often Jesus referred to God as the disciples' Father:

> But when you pray, go into your [most] private room, and, closing the door, pray to your **Father**, Who is in secret; and your **Father**, Who sees in secret, will reward you in the open.
>
> *Matthew 6:6, AMPC*

> If you, then, though you are evil, know how to give good gifts to your children, how much more will your **Father** in heaven give good gifts to those who ask him!
>
> *Matthew 7:11*

> If a son shall ask bread of any of you that is a father, will he give him a stone? or if he ask a fish, will he for a fish give him a serpent? Or if he shall ask an egg, will he offer him a scorpion? If ye then, being evil, know how to give good gifts unto your children: how much more shall your heavenly **Father** give the Holy Spirit to them that ask him?
>
> *Luke 11:11-13, KJV*

John chapter 17 contains Christ's longest prayer, but look at the way He began: "**Father**, the hour has come..." (*John17:1*). He followed this up by saying, "And now, **Father**, glorify me in your presence" (*John 17:5*). He then called upon His "Holy **Father**" (*John 17:11*) to protect the disciples, "that all of them may be one, **Father**, just as you are in me and I am in you" (*John 17:21*), adding, "**Father**, I want those you have given me to be with me where I am..." (*John 17:24*). He concluded His prayer by again addressing God as "Righteous **Father**" (*John 17:25*).

Notice how often He used the same word, "Father"—because He lived with this "Father-Son" consciousness in Him. He used two adjectives to describe God: holy and righteous. But He still ended up using the word "Father".

Every single request that came from His lips in this prayer was answered. If you want to get the same results as Jesus did, if you want to have your Lazarus back, you need to approach God's throne with this consciousness that He is your Father and you are His child. You will not only please Him with such a mindset, but you will also build up your faith as you pray to Him.

A Thankful Heart

"Father, I thank you..." (*John 11:41*).

Here's another reason why His prayer brought Lazarus from the grave: *thankfulness.* First, He entered God's presence with a Father-Son consciousness. But that wasn't all; He entered with a heart full of thanks.

Notice that Jesus had a very big request to make, but He didn't just jump into asking. He showed God that He appreciated all He had done in the past. I am sure God would be nodding His head and saying, "Yes, I'm a good Father"!

Think about this: what if your son comes to you to ask for his school fees, and the first thing he says is, "Father, I want to thank you for paying last term's school fees and for paying my school fees regularly, even when times are hard." How would that make you feel? Won't it make you want to do more for this sensible and grateful child? Jesus understood this principle and applied it in His prayer.

A friend of mine told me he was moved when his son came to him and thanked him for paying his school fees. The boy was grateful because he had seen how other children were sent home when their parents failed to pay the fees on time, and he realized that he too would have been among them if his father had not paid the school fees promptly.

Parents go through a lot. Many times, my parents had to give their last dime just to see that we were comfortable. The best way that children can reciprocate their parents' love is by showing appreciation. The same applies to God. The Bible says He never slumbers nor sleeps (*Psalm 121:4*). He is a watchman whose eyes "run to and fro throughout the whole earth, to show Himself strong on behalf of those whose heart is loyal to Him" (*2 Chronicles 16:9, NKJV*).

He is a merciful Father, ever willing to forgive us our sins. Many times, we don't even realize the battles He fights on our behalf to keep us alive and to deliver us from the clutches of the wicked one. But when we enter His presence, all we have is a load of requests and complaints. And He may just be saying to Himself, "What kind of child is this? Yesterday I saved him from untimely death, but he didn't even mention it. I healed her son, and not even a word of thanks from her. I have kept their marriage from sinking and not even a mention of it…"

When Jesus healed those nine lepers, He waited for them to come and thank Him, but only one showed up. Imagine if the leprosy returned to the eight. What would they do then? They would simply return to Jesus and ask for healing all over again! No expression of gratitude, but they expected the Father to be happy with them.

Jesus lived with a thankful disposition and entered God's presence with reasons to be grateful to Him. Sometimes His prayer was purely to say, "Father, thank you!" No requests. No demands. Just to show His gratitude.

> At that time Jesus answered and said, "I thank You, Father, Lord of heaven and earth, that You have hidden these things from the wise and prudent and have revealed them to babes. Even so, Father, for so it seemed good in Your sight.
>
> *Matthew 11:25-26, NKJV*

Look at His prayer. It was a flow of thankfulness. He didn't question God for revealing those things to "babes"; in fact, He thanked God even more, "for so it seemed good" in His sight. Today we live in a world where ingratitude reigns, because people have bought into the belief that "they owe me a duty": "It's the government's duty to protect me and provide me with the basic amenities"; "It's my husband's duty to meet my needs as a wife"; "It's my parents' duty to look after my welfare, and it's simply normal if they do anything good for me." We have carried this mindset over into our relationship with God, and this is reflected in our prayers: "It's my right as a child of God to receive all His blessings." But we hardly ever think that it is also wise of us to at least say, "Father, I appreciate what you are doing for me as your child."

Jesus had a dead and stinking Lazarus to handle, but that did not stop Him from approaching God with a thankful heart. As it says in *Psalm 100:4*, "Enter his gates with thanksgiving and his courts with praise; give thanks to him and praise his name."

A thankful disposition is an indication of how you view God. It shows that you consider Him to be a good Father—in spite of your circumstances. As the Psalmist puts it: "*Give thanks* to the LORD, for he *is* good; his love endures forever" (*Psalm 107:1*). When you live like Jesus in the realm of thankfulness, you are saying to God: "This marriage may not be what I had hoped for, but it doesn't change the fact that you are a good God. The bills are piling up, but it doesn't change the fact that you are a good Father. There may be some delay, but it doesn't change the fact that you are a good and reliable Father."

Reaffirming this view, Paul exhorts us to ""*give thanks in all circumstances*" for this is God's will for us in Christ Jesus (*1 Thessalonians 5:18*); adding that we should, in every situation we find ourselves in, present our requests to God "by prayer and petition, *with thanksgiving*" (*Philippians 4:6*).

God isn't only interested in your present needs; He's also interested in what you have to say about how He met your previous needs. He doesn't just want to hear about the enemies that are fighting you; He also wants you to talk about the enemies He has saved you from. He doesn't just want you to pray for a new car; He also wants you to talk about the numerous times He delivered you and your present car from accidents and other calamities on the highway. He doesn't just want you to ask Him to save you from those miscarriages, He also wants to hear you talk about the loving husband and the nice home He has given you. No, He doesn't just want you to accuse Him of not giving you a job immediately you left school; He also wants to hear you talk about the fact that you have graduated, when many of your childhood friends never made it this far.

A thankful heart opens doors. Have you been talking to God with an ungrateful heart, whining about your Lazarus? It's time to go into the Father's presence and begin to pay your debt of thanks. You have probably engaged in prayer and supplication but left out thanksgiving; it's time to change your disposition. Be thankful: "giving joyful thanks to the Father, who has qualified you to share in the inheritance of his holy people in the kingdom of light" (*Colossians 1:12*).

The Father's Will

> "And I know that You always hear Me, but because of the people who are standing by I said this, that they may believe that You sent Me."
>
> *John 11:42, NKJV*

The third thing I want us to notice is that Christ wrapped His request around the will of God. The Bible tells us that, if we ask anything according to God's will, He will hear and answer us:

> This is the confidence we have in approaching God: that if we ask anything according to his will, he hears us. And if we know that he hears us—whatever we ask—we know that we have what we asked of him.
>
> *1 John 5:14-15*

Asking according to God's will brings us confidence; when we pray according to God's will, faith springs up in our hearts because we are assured of His answer.

If my three-year-old son were to ask me for a car today, I wouldn't buy it for him even if I had the means. But if He asked me for a textbook that would help him come first in his class, I would grant his request without thinking twice.

The second request is in line with my will for him, because I know how vital it is to his future. Similarly, God has a specific will for each of His children, and we need to align ourselves with His will when we come before Him in prayer. Christ employed this same approach. He didn't just make a request; His request was tied to His Father's will.

For many, many years God promised His children that a Saviour would come. Moses spoke about His coming. Isaiah and other prophets of old spoke about His coming. Many waited for His arrival until they died. But there was this generation that finally saw Him as the Word that became flesh (*John 1:14*). The prophecies and the promises became flesh. But instead of accepting and believing in Him as the Saviour, they dismissed Him as being only "the carpenter's son"—born, they thought, of ordinary parents whom they knew so well! So, they challenged His authority and treated Him with disdain. With this kind of attitude, it was going to be very hard for God's will to prevail—God's will for them to know Him as the only true God and Jesus Christ as the One He had sent (*John 17:5*).

So, when Christ stood at the tomb of Lazarus, He linked His request to this earnest desire in God's heart "that they may believe that you sent me" (*John 11:42*). In essence, He was saying to the Father, "Bring Lazarus back to life, so that these people will believe in you—and in me, whom you have sent. Bring him back to life, so that the Jews and the rest of the world will know that I am not just a prophet, but the Way, the Truth and the Life. Let them see the dead come to life and believe that I have come from you to save them... for no man can do these miracles, except God be with him."

It was a prayer that God was ready to answer, because it was in line with His will. Jesus told the disciples to pray that God's will be done on earth (*Matthew 6:10*). You have a role to play in bringing this about—that God's will may indeed be done on earth—by praying according to His will.

God has a specific will concerning every aspect of your life. He has a specific will concerning your marriage… your finances… your health… your life after death. And He wants that will to be done on earth. It is up to you to pray in line with His will because, when you do so, you can be assured that your prayers will be heard.

The problem with many people is that they do not know God's will for their lives, so it's hard for them to pray in line with it. How do you find God's will for your life? You need to look in His Word: for His will is in His Word. The Bible is a compendium of God's will for man. Jesus went to the synagogue one day and, after reading from *Isaiah 61*, He told the people, "Today this scripture is fulfilled in your hearing" (*Luke 4:21*). He found God's will for His ministry right there in that passage of Scripture.

If you are looking for God's will for your marriage, you won't find it in a biology textbook. If you are looking for His will as to who to marry, you won't find it in a romance novel or a soap opera. If you are looking for His will concerning your health, you won't find it in the doctor's report. If you are looking for His will concerning your future, you won't find it in a newspaper. You will only find His will in His Word. When you find His will for your life, and you pray in line with it, you too will begin to say, "Father I thank You because you always hear me."

Discovering God's will for you keeps you from asking amiss; as James said, "You ask and do not receive, because you ask amiss" (*James 4:3, NKJV*). Whatever challenges you are facing, don't rush into God's presence and start weeping and pleading, "Change my story." Take a moment to find out His will for your situation.

To give you an idea of what it means to align yourself with God's will for your situation, let us take the case of a woman who is unable to conceive. The Psalmist assures us, "He maketh the barren woman to keep house and to be a joyful mother of children" (*Psalm 113:9, KJV*). Now, that's God's will for you, if you are a barren woman—and there's a two-fold package in there. Instead of sobbing endlessly and telling God how your friends are talking about you, talk to Him about this two-fold blessing:

Keeping your home. You won't lose your home just because you can't have a baby. I know of women who have lost their husbands and homes because they couldn't give their husbands children. But here God says, "He makes the barren woman to keep house." He preserves your home and marriage from the hussies who are ready to take your place.

A joyful mother of children. It is also God's will to make you a joyful mother of children. I have seen mothers who are not joyful. They are full of sadness, even when they are with their children. God's plan for you, however, is not only to have children but to be a joyful mother.

If you are a wife who is unable to conceive, pray for this two-fold blessing promised to you in *Psalm 113:9*. This is what it means to pray in line with God's will: praying according to His Word. It is the approach that Jesus employed, and it got Him the ear of the Father: "if we ask anything according to his will, he hears us" (*1 John 5:14*).

11

The Power of His Voice

Now when He had said these things, He cried with a loud voice, "Lazarus, come forth!"

John 11:43, NKJV

Men obey voices. Demons obey voices. Situations obey voices. You can enter into bondage by the power of a voice, and you can be set free from that same bondage by the power of a voice. Dead people and dead situations don't come back to life by weeping and human effort; they come back to life by the power of a voice.

The voice of the Lord is the voice that makes everything come alive:

Believe Me when I assure you, most solemnly I tell you, the time is coming and is here now when the dead shall hear the voice of the Son of God and those who hear it shall live.

John 5:25, AMPC

Dead wombs hear the voice of the Lord and come alive. Dead marriages hear the voice of the Lord and come alive. Dead businesses hear the voice of the Lord and come alive. Dead careers hear the voice of the Lord and come alive. Dead dreams hear the voice of the Lord and come alive. Dead projects hear the voice of the Lord and come alive.

Dead relationships hear the voice of the Lord and come alive. Dead churches and ministries hear the voice of the Lord and come alive. Dead Lazarus heard the voice of the Lord and came back to life. Your dead or ailing problem can equally hear the voice of the Lord and come alive.

His Voice Reigns Supreme over All Creation

The voice of a president carries weight only within the borders of his own country; his power and authority are limited to his own nation. So too is the voice of a father limited to his own family, and the voice of a teacher to his own students. But the voice of the Lord knows no boundary or limit.

> Hear attentively the thunder of His voice, and the rumbling that comes from His mouth.
>
> He sends it forth under the whole heaven, His lightning to the ends of the earth.
>
> *Job 37:2-3, NKJV*

> The voice of the LORD is over the waters; the God of glory thunders; the LORD is over many waters.
>
> *Psalm 29:3, NKJV*

It doesn't matter if the forces that come against you are in or beneath the sea. They will hear and obey the voice of the Lord. It doesn't matter if the powers working against you are in a planet far away from the earth. They will hear and obey the voice of the Lord. Wherever evil powers have converged to conspire against you, His voice is able to penetrate and reverse their resolutions. His voice reaches out to the ends of the earth and beyond.

His Voice Makes Unbelievable Things Happen

God thunders marvelously with His voice; He does great things which we cannot comprehend.

Job 37:5, NKJV

Unbelievable things happen when the voice of the Lord thunders. Only the voice of the Lord can bring to life a dead and stinking body. *The voice of the Lord does great things which we cannot comprehend.* When all hope seemed lost, whose voice parted the Red Sea, paving the way for God's children to cross over? *The voice of the Lord does great things which we cannot comprehend.*

Are people saying that you can't get a job because you don't have "connections"? *The voice of the Lord does great things which we cannot comprehend.* The voice of the Lord can give you a plum job and cause people to wonder, "How did you get it?" Have the doctors pronounced you as incapable of having children? You can be a proud parent in nine months. *The voice of the Lord does great things which we cannot comprehend.* Have your family and community written you off as a "mere dreamer"? The same people who wrote you off will come and bow before you. *The voice of the Lord does great things which we cannot comprehend.*

I wonder what evil name or label you have been saddled with—whether in your church, family, or place of work, for any reason whatsoever. You won't be going to the grave with that label. *The voice of the Lord does great things which we cannot comprehend.* Get ready to see the impossible become possible in your life, because that's what the voice of the Lord does.

The Voice of the Lord is a Voice of Power

> The voice of the LORD is powerful; the voice of the LORD is majestic.
>
> The voice of the LORD breaks the cedars; the LORD breaks in pieces the cedars of Lebanon.
>
> He makes Lebanon leap like a calf, Sirion like a young wild ox.
>
> *Psalm 29:4*

You think you have powerful enemies? The voice of the Lord is your weapon of warfare. It is a voice of power. Whatever evil pronouncements your enemies have made against you, whatever voices they have raised against you that might be affecting your progress and success in life, there is a voice more powerful than theirs: it is the voice of the Lord.

It is a voice so powerful that, just as it broke the mighty cedars of Lebanon, it can break whatever needs to be broken in your life and give you your full restoration. It is a voice that can put all your enemies to flight; He will make them "leap like a calf" and "like a young wild ox" as they scatter in fright—just as He did with Israel's enemies.

His Voice Restores

> He shouted with a loud voice, Lazarus, come out! And out walked the man who had been dead...
>
> *John 11:43-44, AMPC*

The voice of the Lord restores. The moment it spoke, Lazarus couldn't stay in the grave for another minute. Every debate and argument in the realm of the spirit ceased; they had to let him go. I see the same happening in your life now.

The devil is letting go of all the things he has taken from you. Everything changed, the very moment the voice of the Lord spoke. Rejoice, for the voice of the Lord is changing your story this moment. Amen.

The Operation of His Voice

The voice of the Lord operates in various ways to bring us victory. I will touch on just four of these ways:

The independent voice of the Lord

I term it independent because it does not rely on any medium to find expression. It is God's direct voice—the voice of the Father, Son or Holy Spirit. This is the voice that spoke in Genesis chapter 1: the voice that spoke at creation. The voice that said, "Let there be light," and there was light; the voice that said, "Let the water teem with living creatures" (*Genesis 1:20*) and it was so.

This independent voice is the voice that calls things into existence. It can call into existence your marriage; it can call into existence new body parts if you need some. This was the voice that called Lazarus out of the grave, and death couldn't hold him back. I see this voice speaking into your life and your situation.

This direct voice of the Lord is audible to our physical ears. It was audible to Adam and Eve. It was audible to Moses. It was audible to Jesus and those who were with Him at certain points in His ministry. It is also audible in our day but, in most cases, our ear may not hear the expressions of this direct voice. Only on rare occasions will our physical ears hear this direct voice.

It is comforting to note that, when we pray, or when we worship God or take a step of faith, this direct voice of the Lord finds expression. Though our physical ears may not hear His voice, the events that occur thereafter point to the fact that it is at work. When the voice of the Lord speaks, the kingdom of darkness hears Him and they obey.

The prison foundations shook, the doors flew open and the captives' chains were loosened when Saul and Silas praised God (*Acts 16:25-26*). The place responded to the voice of the Lord.

The representative voice of the Lord

I call it representative because here the voice of the Lord finds expression through a medium. It could be a human medium, an angelic medium, or even an animal—as in the case of Balaam (*Numbers 22:28-30*). Rather than speaking directly, God finds a medium through which His voice is expressed.

There may be times when the president of a country is expected to make a speech but, for some reason or other, is not around in person. On such occasions, representatives may be sent to stand in for the president. Such representatives do not speak in their own capacity; they speak as the voice of the president. Their words and actions are considered to be those of the president.

The same applies to the representative voice of God. Our God-ordained pastors, ministers and church leaders are God's representatives. When they say, "You are blessed," it is God who is saying, "You are blessed." Rejoice! When they say that you are healed or set free, believe it and rejoice. It is God who is speaking.

I am the LORD, the Maker of all things... who carries out the words of his servants and fulfils the predictions of his messengers...

Isaiah 44: 24, 26

Believe in the LORD your God, and you shall be established; believe His prophets, and you shall prosper.

2 Chronicles 20:20, NKJV

Those who saw Jesus growing up did not believe in Him. Don't make the same mistake they did. "Who is he?" they queried. "Isn't that the carpenter's son? Isn't that the guy who made our dining table? We know His brothers and sisters. We know when He was born. We attended the same school. Where did He get His authority from? We can't honour Him. We can't be His followers." They missed out on the blessings of God because they didn't realize God had made Jesus His Representative Voice.

Samuel was just one of those boys helping Eli out with the priestly work. But one day he had an encounter with God and God made him His representative voice. The Bible tells us that, from that time onwards, "The LORD was with Samuel as he grew up, and he let none of Samuel's words fall to the ground" (*1 Samuel 3:19*).

The Lord was with Samuel, and He fulfilled all of Samuel's predictions. Here was a true representative of God! But not everyone who claims to be God's servant or messenger is really from Him. That is why we sometimes hear "prophecies"—purportedly from God—that never come true, and then we start wondering: "But God said...!" At other times, those giving the "prophecies" may be true servants of God, but what they are saying may not have come from God; it may have come from themselves.

Therefore thus says the Lord concerning the [false] prophets who prophesy in My name—although I did not send them—and who say, Sword and famine shall not be in this land: By sword and famine shall those prophets be consumed.

Jeremiah 14:15, AMPC

Then Jeremiah said to Hananiah, the false prophet, "Listen, Hananiah, the Lord has not sent you..."

Jeremiah 28:15, TLB

Jesus had a different result as God's representative voice, because He received His words from the Father:

But He Who sent Me is true... and I tell the world [only] the things that I have heard from Him... I do nothing of Myself (of My own accord or on My own authority), but I say [exactly] what My Father has taught Me.

John 8: 26, 28, AMPC

I have never spoken on My own authority or of My own accord or as self-appointed, but the Father Who sent Me has Himself given Me orders [concerning] what to say and what to tell.

John 12:49, AMPC

He spoke only the words that came from God, so His words were with power—because "the voice of the LORD is powerful" (*Psalm 29:4*). And the people were astounded:

Then they were all amazed, so that they questioned among themselves, saying, "What is this? What new doctrine is this? For with authority He commands even the unclean spirits, and they obey Him."

Mark 1:27, NKJV

What they were seeing was the voice of God in operation. The representative voice of God is powerful; it can bring forth your Lazarus.

The authorized voice of the Lord

To authorize is to give official permission to somebody to do or say something. There are times when God authorizes another person to speak on His behalf, and the voice of this other person is as effective as the direct voice of God. The first man to enjoy this privilege was Adam:

> Out of the ground the LORD God formed every beast of the field and every bird of the air, and brought them to Adam to see what he would call them. And whatever Adam called each living creature, that was its name.
>
> *Genesis 2:19, NKJV*

Notice the last part of the verse: "whatever Adam called each living creature, that was its name". God didn't make any alteration. The angels and demons raised no objection, because Adam's voice was God's authorized voice. As Adam gave each creature its name, God went ahead to put His seal on it. It was as good as God naming them Himself.

What is most interesting is that believers in the New Testament can equally enjoy what Adam did. When Jesus said to His disciples, "whatever you bind on earth will be bound in heaven, and whatever you loose on earth will be loosed in heaven" (*Matthew 18:18*), He was telling them that God had made them His authorized voice.

Born again Christians have the authorized voice of God. That was why Paul could say to Elymas the sorcerer, "You are going to be blind for a time, not even able to see the light of the sun," and it happened exactly as Paul had said.

Acts 13:11 tells us that "immediately mist and darkness came over him, and he groped about, seeking someone to lead him by the hand". Why? Because Paul spoke as God's authorized voice, and God gave His consent for it to happen.

There is, as you have probably noticed, a distinction between God's representative voice and His authorized voice. As God's representative voice, you are required to speak the words you receive from Him. As His authorized voice, you have the privilege of speaking for yourself; and though what you have said may not necessarily be what you have heard from Him, He puts His seal on it.

When God took Ezekiel to the valley of dry bones, He could have brought life to those dead bones through His independent voice. Instead, He told Ezekiel, His representative voice, to speak to those dry bones on His behalf. Ezekiel got results because he said what he heard from God:

> Then he told me to speak to the bones and say: "O dry bones, listen to the words of God, for the Lord God says, 'See! I am going to make you live and breathe again! I will replace the flesh and muscles on you and cover you with skin. I will put breath into you, and you shall live and know I am the Lord.'"
>
> So I spoke these words from God, just as he told me to; and suddenly there was a rattling noise from all across the valley, and the bones of each body came together and attached to each other as they used to be.
>
> *Ezekiel 37:4-7, TLB*

Ezekiel spoke the words he received from God—as His representative voice. On the other hand, we see how Jesus spoke to the man with the unclean spirit in the synagogue, saying, "Be quiet, and come out of him!" (*Mark 1:25, NKJV*).

Here, He was speaking as God's authorized voice. And in *Mark 4:39*, when He spoke to the storm, He was again speaking as God's authorized voice—and the sea obeyed Him the same way it would obey God the Father. That made the disciples marvel!

Note that Jesus in the course of His ministry on earth operated in all three ways: as the *independent* voice of God (because, of course, He was God Himself); as God's *representative voice*; and as the *authorised* voice of the Lord.

Today we are immensely privileged as God's children to be able to operate as His authorised voice—like Jesus did— and win the battles of life. God is waiting for you to speak so that He can put His seal on what you say. Demons are not going to say, "That's the voice of Brother (or Sister) So-and-so." They are going to say, "That's the voice of the Lord"—because it carries His seal. Glory to God.

The documented voice of the Lord

The Bible is God's documented voice. It is a compilation of His spoken words, documented by holy men who were inspired by the Holy Spirit. In other words, they wrote what they heard: "The whole Bible was given to us by inspiration from God" (*2 Timothy 3:16, TLB*).

> For no prophecy recorded in Scripture was ever thought up by the prophet himself. It was the Holy Spirit within these godly men who gave them true messages from God.
>
> *2 Peter 1:20-21, TLB*

The Bible is not subject to review. Some people want us to review the Bible the way we review the constitution, so that it will *meet modern demands.* Sorry, it cannot be reviewed.

It is forever settled in heaven—not on earth. (*Psalm 119:89*). You either take it as it is or leave it. The moment you subject it to review to "meet our modern demands", it ceases to be the voice of God; it becomes the voice of man and thereby loses its potency. It is the voice of God, not the voice of man.

There is today a proliferation of men's voices disguised as the voice of God—which is why we are getting so little in the way of results. But the true voice of God is powerful. And it is timeless (*Isaiah 40:8; Matthew 24:35*). It is as powerful as it was two thousand years ago. It has the capacity to do what it did two thousand years ago. It is no respecter of age or race. What it did in Israel thousands of years ago, it can also do in your country today. The documented voice of God can work for you now and restore your Lazarus. Get a hold of it and say to your Lazarus, "Hear, hear the voice of the Lord!" Mention your case and declare what the voice of God has to say about it.

The Operation of His Voice in Your Life

There's no need for you to say, "I wish Jesus were right here to address my problem the way He addressed Martha's." No! The voice of the Lord is right here with you now: *His Independent Voice, His Representative Voice, His Authorized Voice,* and *His Documented Voice.*

Using the medium of this book, I hereby decree, as the representative voice of the Lord, that you now receive the solution to every problem you are facing, in Jesus' Name! I speak into every area where you have experienced shame and defeat. Rise up in victory; let there be a restoration of all that the devil has taken from you, in Jesus' name! Amen.

12

A Glorious End

And out walked the man who had been dead…

John 11:44, AMPC

God is not only interested in the beginning of a matter; He is also interested in the end of it. For God's children, the beginning doesn't necessarily determine the end: "Though your beginning was small, yet your latter end should greatly increase" (*Job 8:7, AKJV*). For Lazarus, it began with sickness and then temporary death. But there is a God who determines the end from the beginning. He determined the end of Lazarus' problem when He declared, "This sickness will not end in death" (*John 11:4*).

> I am God, and there is none like me, declaring the end from the beginning, and from ancient times the things that are not yet done, saying, My counsel shall stand, and I will do all my pleasure…
> *Isaiah 46:9-10, KJV*

You may be weeping at the moment, but God has prepared a glorious end for you. Like Mary and Martha, you may not know the full details of what He has planned, but take heart because He has promised to give you "hope and a future" (*Jeremiah 29:11*).

As we come to the conclusion of this great resurrection story, I want to point out two things that you should expect when Jesus, the Omega, restores your Lazarus.

119

A Change of Garment

> And out walked the man who had been dead, his hands and feet wrapped in burial cloths... Jesus said to them, Free him of the burial wrappings and let him go.
>
> *John 11:44, AMPC*

Lazarus had on him "burial cloths", but he received a change of garment the moment Jesus stepped in and uttered the word of life. I don't know the garment you are wearing right now. Some are wearing the garment of failure. They are hardly successful in anything they do, because the wicked one has clothed them with the garment of failure.

Some are wearing the garment of sickness. The enemy never gives them a break; just as they are recovering from one illness, the devil puts another on them. And they are heavily in debt from having to pay all those medical bills. For others, it is the garment of rejection. Everywhere they go, no one seems to get along with them. They have lost relationships and opportunities because, unknown to them, they are wearing the garment of rejection.

Jesus made sure that Lazarus not only came back to life, but he was freed from the burial wrappings which had held him bound for four days. Expect the Lord to also remove every evil garment you are now wearing: garments of broken relationships, barrenness, failure, misfortune, joblessness, shame, and untimely death.

In *Isaiah 61:3*, God promised His children a change of garment: "a garment of praise instead of a spirit of despair". I see your garment changing. God is removing that evil garment which has caused you untold sorrow, and He's replacing it with a garment of praise.

An End to Stagnation

Jesus said to them, Free him of the burial wrappings and let him go.

John 11:44, AMPC

When Jesus gives the word of life, expect stagnation to end. Lazarus came out bound, unable to move. He was alive, but he wasn't making any progress. His life remained in a spot. Jesus didn't like that; He made sure Lazarus was set free so that he could go and accomplish God's plan for his life.

Perhaps you are stagnating too: you established that business five years ago, but it's almost like you just started. You've worked for 35 years, but those who started a year ago are faring better than you. That relationship is seven years old, but you are still not sure if it will end in marriage. Something is wrong. The enemy wants you to remain in a spot.

Jesus refused to let Lazarus remain in a spot. It was great he had come out of the grave. It was great he was alive. But God wanted him to have more. God doesn't just want you to be alive, He also wants you to make progress. Remaining in a spot is not His wish for you.

You have stayed long enough at this mountain... Go in and take possession of the land the LORD swore he would give to your fathers—to Abraham, Isaac and Jacob—and to their descendants after them.

Deuteronomy 1: 6, 8

The powers holding and keeping you in a spot will hear the voice of the Lord and let you go. It's your season to make progress; the Lord is breaking the yoke of stagnation in your life today, and from this moment you will go forth and possess all that He has prepared for you. Amen.

www.ingramcontent.com/pod-product-compliance
Lightning Source LLC
Chambersburg PA
CBHW071757150726
47998CB00005B/1972